Mackenzie King's

GHOST

and other personal accounts
of Canadian hauntings

Mackenzie King's
GHOST

—————— ◆ ——————

and other personal accounts of Canadian hauntings

JOHN ROBERT COLOMBO

HOUNSLOW

Dedication
For Iris and George Owen

Mackenzie King's Ghost
and Other Personal Accounts of Canadian Hauntings

Copyright © 1991 by J.R. Colombo

Second Printing, June 1991

All Rights Reserved.

ISBN 0-88882-136-0

Publisher: Anthony Hawke
Designer: Gerard Williams
Compositor: Accurate Typesetting Limited
Printer: Gagné Printing Ltd.
Front Cover Photograph: Bill Brooks

Page 190 constitutes
an extension of the copyright page.

Publication was assisted by
the Canada Council and the
Ontario Arts Council.

Hounslow Press
A Division of Anthony R. Hawke Limited
124 Parkview Avenue
Willowdale, Ontario, Canada M2N 3Y5

Printed and bound in Canada.

Contents

Preface

Do ghosts exist? Are houses haunted? Can the dead communicate with the living? Are there places that should be shunned? And one final question: Did Mackenzie King's ghost appear to Percy J. Philip one sunny afternoon in June 1954, while the veteran Ottawa correspondent for *The New York Times* was relaxing on a park bench at Kingsmere — despite the fact that at the time the former Prime Minister of Canada had been dead for four years?

Instead of considering questions like these, *Mackenzie King's Ghost* offers the reader true tales of Canadian hauntings. These first-person, eye-witness accounts are presented as fact, not fiction. Here are fifty, real-life ghost stories — evocations of ghosts and spirits, spectres and apparitions, poltergeists and other peculiar presences. Such mysterious beings haunt the pages of this book.

Here is a national gallery of familiar and not-so-familiar ghosts: The spirit of a soldier saves the life of his Canadian brother-at-arms at Vimy…a lantern-carrying spectre stalks a student through the rooms of an abandoned hotel…a scent mysteriously lingers in the house of a distinguished author…a poltergeist snores and keeps everyone awake in a bungalow in the interior of British Columbia…the silhouette of a woman appears and reappears in a root cellar…a beautiful Lady in White flits from one old Ontario stone house to another in search of her long-dead husband…a lighthouse on Georgian Bay has most peculiar bannisters…a large,

1

egg-shaped object glows in a bedroom...an evil presence lurks up the attic stairs...the spectre of a black, howling wolf reappears...a schoolhouse in Edmonton is haunted...a streetlamp mysteriously blinks answers to questions about a dead girl...a "sticky man" lurks in the cellar....

The argument that Canada is too young a country to have hosts of ghosts is hoary with age. The statement itself is more than a century and a half old. The pioneer author Catharine Parr Traill wrote in 1836: "As to ghosts and spirits, they appear totally banished from Canada. This is too matter-of-fact a country for such supernaturals to visit." Her brother, Samuel Strickland, another pioneer author, added for good measure in 1853: "The country is too new for such gentry."

The country's woodlands and waterways held no mysteries for pioneers like Mrs. Traill and Major Strickland. Had they been responsive to the real nature of their adopted land, such settlers would have discerned in the deep woods the dark outlines of the Indian's Windigo and in the deep northern waters the watery shadows of the Inuit's Sedna.

"It's only by our lack of ghosts we're haunted," the poet Earle Birney suggested as late as 1962. In Canada today there may be no equivalent of London's Black Tower, Borley Rectory in Essex, or Forfarshire's Glamis Castle, each with its long and bloody history, so ghastly and so ghostly. But what we lack in castles we more than make up in lurking presences. This "dark dominion" of ours has its own gallery of ghosts. To see them all we have to do is recognize that they are there. Only then will we be able to deal with their presences and manifestations. The need is there. As Robertson Davies stated in 1982, "Canada needs ghosts, as a dietary supplement, a vitamin taken to stave off that most dreadful of modern ailments, the Rational Rickets."

The accounts of ghosts and hauntings in this book may or may not stave off "the Rational Rickets." Ten of the accounts are reprinted from the pages of old books, magazines, newspapers, and journals. Forty accounts derive from private correspondence. Whenever I appear as a guest on a radio show or television program, I invite listeners or viewers to contact me about their extraordinary experiences. Many do. Indeed, ten accounts in the present book are based on correspondence following media contact. The remaining thirty accounts are based on correspondence with newspaper readers who responded to my letters to editors requesting "ghost stories" for use in future books.

From time to time readers and reviewers of my earlier collections, *Extraordinary Experiences* and *Mysterious Encounters*, have asked me the following interesting question: "What steps have you taken to check the authenticity of the accounts that are selected for publication?" My reply runs like this: "There is no way to prove that these episodes actually occurred. How can anyone check an *experience*? It is difficult enough to determine that an *event* took place. Surely what is most important is that the episode, whether a subjective experience or an objective event, is described with candour and explained in a mysterious manner."

So the reader is asked to accept the words of the informants at face value. This is not always easy to do. I have no problem with the integrity of the informants whose accounts appear in this book. I trust that they are sincere in what they have written. From time to time I want to point out to them that there are plausible explanations for what has been described. At other times I am at a loss to offer any explanation at all for what has happened, but I am aware of the fact that accounts are based on memory and that memory is not immune to the effects of fabrication, confabulation, and imagination.

One step I did take was to draft a memorandum and request that each informant sign it. The memorandum, called a "Note of Assurance," makes the following points in the first person:

> The events and experiences are true to my recollections of them and true to my reconstructions of them.
>
> All relevant details are included. No fictitious details are included.
>
> The account is offered to the public and for publication with no intent to deceive. I wrote it to draw attention to events and experiences that have occurred to me.

The memorandum was signed by everyone to whom it was offered. All the correspondents whose letters appear in this book signed it.

What should the reader make of these accounts? What do they tell us about people and about mysterious presences and powers? To answer those questions, it is useful to consider the difference between an *account* and a *report*. The word *account* refers to a first-person narrative; the word *report* is reserved for a second-hand description like an article about a haunting or an interview with a witness written by a non-participant like a newspaper reporter. Only accounts appear in this book, no reports.

My preferred term for an account or first-person narrative is a *memorate*. The Swedish scholar C.W. von Sydow introduced this term into folklore studies for what he calls a "narrative of a personal happening." Such narratives are often called "belief tales" because such tales "give credence to folk beliefs," as Jan Harold Brunvand, the American collector of urban legends, expressed it in *The Study of American Folklore* (3rd edition, 1986). Neither von Sydow nor Brunvand restricts the use of the word *memorate* to "the mysterious." But for the purposes of this book, a memorate is a personal experience narrative with a strong element of the mysterious. The following definition may prove to be useful:

> A *memorate* is a truthful account of an anomalous event or experience, oral in origin, narrative in form, expressed in the first person, related to sympathetic people by the person to whom the episode occurred, made especially significant and meaningful through the inclusion of elements that are both ordinary and outlandish, and concluding with an expression of the realization that the episode is contrary to common sense, to science, and to consensual reality.

Memorates are at once informal and formulaic. They are informal in expression because kinship or friendship is implied in the sharing of intimate experiences that are not easily shared with strangers. They are formulatic in the sense that, at least abstractly, they begin and end in ways that are highly formalized. A memorate might begin with words like these: "Some time ago something odd happened to me." It might end like this: "That is what happened to me and to this day I do not know what to make of it."

My use of a term from the discipline of folklore to refer to these first-person narratives is not meant to imply that the events and experiences that they relate are imaginary. Memorates are not records of myths, legends, or folktales. Instead, my use of a folkloristic term is meant to suggest that memorates form a distinct class of prose narratives. If this class has a function, it is to familiarize the unfamiliar. Memorates make known to oneself and to others the effect or effects of the unknown on the life of the narrator. Although memorates call into question the operation of cause and effect in the world as we know it, they assert that the world is not as we know it and that now and then some little-known or unknown form of cause and effect occasionally takes effect. The lives of many of the informants have been enriched and enlarged by their bizarre experiences, but it must be stated that the lives of some others have been blighted and diminished by such experiences. Psychological pressures are released through the relating of these episodes. It is not farfetched to suggest, as well, that the same relief is experienced by the listener or the reader of these accounts. To put it briefly, while ghosts may distill fear, ghost stories siphon it off.

Did the episodes described in these memorates really occur? Do ghosts exist in any objective sense? If so, do they violate the conventions of consensus reality? Even asking such questions seems silly as Samuel Johnson once observed, "It is wonderful that five thousand years have not elapsed since the creation of the world, and still it is undecided whether or not there has ever been an instance of the spirit of any person appearing after death. All argument is against it; but all belief is for it."

Dr. Johnson's observation was recorded by James Boswell on April 3, 1778. Twelve days later, the Good Doctor assured his biographer Boswell that the question of the existence of ghosts and spirits was not a frivolous one but remained "whether in theology or philosophy, one of the most important that can come before the human understanding."

To this day Johnson's question, as important as it may be, remains undecided. This development or lack of development is surprising when one considers the activities of investigators throughout the 19th and 20th centuries: thousands of seances sponsored by spiritualists; millions of sittings and readings held by mediums and channellers of the so-called New Age; not to mention innumerable experiments conducted in the parapsychology laboratories of colleges and universities in many countries. Dr. Johnson would find all the inconclusive activity "wonderful."

My work on these memorates — collecting, discussing, reading, editing, keyboarding, studying, comparing, contrasting, and pondering the implications of these accounts and hundreds more like them in my files — has led me to the conclusion that they tell us more about human nature than they do about non-human nature. Another way of expressing this conclusion is to note that these memorates shed more light on *psychical* matters than they do on *psychic* matters.

It has been said that "experience is the best experiment." I am frequently asked the question, "Do you believe in ghosts?" My standard reply goes like this: "Ghosts belong to the category of experience, not belief." There is no actual proof of the operation of the paranormal, but there is some evidence for it. Almost all of that evidence is anecdotal like these memorates. There is now a long history of psychical research and parapsychology that can be studied to great effect. Perhaps the research will tell us something about psychic effects which, to judge by these accounts, seem to occur spontaneously and sporadically. By studying such accounts we may try to understand how human beings come to terms with the mysteries that exist in terms of the lives that they lead. The history of ghosts and poltergeists is a history rich in dramatic instances of access and accommodation.

One way to make room for the mysterious in everyday life involves the telling of stories. Perhaps the fact that these memorates are such good stories — engrossing, hair-raising — is of paramount importance. Story-telling, far from being peripheral to human nature, meets deep-seated personal and communal needs.

The Swiss analyst Carl Jung speculated on the status of the supernatural and held strong opinions about the usefulness of research into the nature of occult studies. His writings in this field are collected in *Psychology and the Occult* (1977), translated by R. F. C. Hull, a volume in Princeton University Press's Bollingen Series. Jung found occasion to quote a passage written by Immanuel Kant which expressed his position with regard to the possibility of acquiring knowledge in the field of psychical research. As the German philosopher explained in his essay "Dreams of a Spirit-Seer" (1766), "The same ignorance makes me so bold as to absolutely deny the truth of the various ghost stories, and yet with the common, although queer, reservation that while I doubt any one of them, still I have a certain faith in the whole of them together." Jung added his approval in the essay "Ghost: False Belief or True" (1950): "One would wish that very many of our bigots would take note of this wise position adopted by a great thinker."

In the essay titled "Apparitions and Precognition" (c.1950), Jung placed such experiences and happenings in the widest of all contexts:

> One doesn't speak of these things, however. They simply happen, and the intellectuals know nothing of them — for intellectuals know neither themselves nor people as they really are. In the world of the latter, without their being conscious of it, the life of the centuries lives on, and things are continually happening that have accompanied human life from time immemorial: premonitions, foreknowledge, second sight, hauntings, ghosts, return of the dead, bewitchings, sorcery, magic, spells, etc.

Jung characterized these manifestations, whatever their causes, as "psychic facts." He noted that it is important that what he called "the *twilight atmosphere* that is so essential to the story is preserved." He added the following warning:

> An integral component of any nocturnal, numinous experience is the dimming of consciousness, the feeling that one is in the grip of something greater than oneself, the impossibility of exercising criticism, and the paralysis of the will. Under the impact of the experience reason evaporates and another power spontaneously takes control — a most singular feeling which one willy-nilly hoards up as a secret treasure no matter how much one person may protest. That, indeed, is the uncomprehended purpose of the experience — to make us feel the overpowering presence of a mystery.

Canadians have been content to be consumers of world mysteries. More specifically, we were content to be connoisseurs of Old World mysteries which came to us from Great Britain, France, and Germany in particular. When we looked over top of our own land, we generally overlooked its most salient features. What we recognized were weak versions or variants of European mysteries and then mysteries imported from the United States. These might be called "branch-plant mysteries."

Yet there are ghosts and spirits (or at least experiences of them) that these are indigenously our own. They cry out for recognition.

Mackenzie King's Ghost is an attempt to draw attention to the ghostly side of Canadian life. One family in particular has made notable contributions to our ghostly lore. With its deep roots in Highland Scotland, the Mackenzie family has added immensely to our national host of ghosts. William Lyon Mackenzie (1795-1861) is recalled as the leader of the reform movement in pre-Confederation Canada. He led the abortive Rebellion of 1837 in Upper Canada, today's Ontario. Historians know him as a man of spirits, not as a spirit! Only lately has his name been linked with an impish spirit — a tiny, bald-headed ghost — which is said to haunt his last earthly residence, Mackenzie House, in downtown Toronto.

The grandson of the rebel leader was William Lyon Mackenzie King (1874-1950), the tenth Prime Minister of Canada. Throughout his life Mackenzie King was fascinated with spiritualism and the "spirit world."

A secretive man by nature, he managed to keep this passion and practices under wraps and far from public knowledge. He was a closet spiritualist. But following his death, the public was made aware of how Mackenzie King had consulted mediums and psychics, visiting them whenever free to do so at home and abroad.

Blair Fraser, the journalist, broke the story with his major article, "The Secret Life of Mackenzie King, Spiritualist," which appeared in *Maclean's* on 15 Dec. 1951. But it was not until scholars were permitted access to the voluminous diaries kept by Mackenzie King throughout his life that the full extent of the late Prime Minister's spiritualistic interests came to light. The military historian C. P. Stacey published a revealing study of the man which showed him to be, from time to time, preoccupied with sex and obsessed with superstitious and spiritualistic practices. *A Very Double Life: The Private World of Mackenzie King* (1976) is Stacey's thorough study of the enigmatic man's attendance at se-ances and even "table-rapping" sessions held at Laurier House in Ottawa and Kingsmere in Gatineau Park. Stacey based his study of the late Prime Minister on the unpublished diaries, but even Stacey, a distinguished military historian, did not have access to every document:

> Some private corresondence and other documents in the King Papers are still closed, including some of the detailed records of King's spiritualistic activities. I am sure that various inves-tigators — not only historians, but political scientists, psy-chologists, psychical researchers, and others — will find in the Papers material to occupy them for generations to come.

So the full story has yet to emerge. Stacey scoffed at the suggestion that "spirit-return" was the explanation for the factual information found in some of the messages that King received from "the beyond." Yet the historian was at a loss to explain the nature of all the communications:

> Where did the references...come from?...The only explana-tion I can offer is that thought-transference in some form took place between King and the medium. It is much easier to believe in this happening between living people than to believe in communication between the dead and the living.

Stacey was prepared to accept some form of telepathy (or perhaps clairvoyance) to account for the factual information that was con-veyed during some of the sittings and sessions.

There is no record in the diaries that Mackenzie King ever saw a ghost. But the spirit-quest met the deep needs of the Prime Minister of Canada as it did of two Prime Ministers of Great Britain, W. E. Gladstone and A. J. Balfour. "Psychic study affords me consider-able relaxation. It is a field of research to which I would devote much time, had I the time to spare," the Canadian Prime Minister wrote in a letter sent from Ottawa on 21 Sept. 1942 to Nandor

Fodor, the respected psychoanalyst and psychical researcher who reproduced their fascinating correspondence in his book of reminiscences, *Between Two Worlds* (1964).

Had Mackenzie King really wanted to encounter a ghost or a spirit, he might well have visited Mackenzie House on a dark and stormy night. Yet he kept the mystical and the material halves of his nature at bay. He was ambivalent about the restoration of his grandfather's residence. Despite his personal wealth, he refused to donate more than good wishes when he was approached for a monetary contribution by T. Wilbur Best, the Toronto antiquarian who established the Mackenzie Homestead Foundation in 1949 to ensure the preservation of the building.

Readers of the present book may well be familiar with the lively poem which is titled "1838." It was written by the poet Dennis Lee and the complete text appears in his book of children's verse, *Nicholas Knock and Other People* (1974). In his poem the poet calls for the return of the spirit of William Lyon Mackenzie. It might even be said that Lee has symbolically summoned up Mackenzie's spirit, though it is doubtful that the poet had in mind the "spirit-return" of Mackenzie when he wrote the poem which concludes with these lines:

> Mackenzie was a crazy man,
> He wrote his wig askew.
> He donned three bulky overcoats
> In case the bullets flew.
> Mackenzie talked of fighting
> While the fight went down the drain.
> But who will speak for Canada?
> Mackenzie, come again!

There are no accounts or reports that suggest that William Lyon Mackenzie has returned to "speak for Canada," although everyone knows the hour is at hand! But some evidence is offered in the pages of *Mackenzie King's Ghost* that on one occasion, at least, in June 1954, the impossible happened...and the spirit of William Lyon Mackenzie King returned to his beloved Kingsmere and talked about "cabbages and kings."

Acknowledgements

To acknowledge is to name...

Much of the research was conducted by the researcher Alice M. Neal at the Metropolitan Toronto Reference Library where the librarians were of considerable assistance. Librarians at the CBC Reference Library in Toronto were unfailingly considerate. Philip Singer and Michael Richardson of the North York Public Library lent a hand with specific queries. Dwight Whalen, writer and researcher, was generous in the extreme, supplying me with much intriguing material gleaned in the Niagara region. Mark Leiren-Young of Vancouver and Eiran Harris, formerly of Vancouver and latterly of Montreal, directed my attention to references I would otherwise have missed. Winnipeg broadcaster and columnist Peter Warren, folklorist Edith Fowke, and sociologist W. Edward (Ted) Mann were of signal assistance. Susan L. Meisner Publicity and Promotion of Toronto handled the bulk mailing of the "ghost letters." Publisher and friend Anthony R. Hawke of Hounslow Press agreed to issue this book; Gerard Williams agreed to design it. The final acknowledgement is due to Ruth Colombo, my wife, for reasons which she knows only too well.

1. Wild Places

L. M. Montgomery

Let us allow L.M. Montgomery to set the scene with an evocation of "Wild Places." Lucy Maud Montgomery (1874-1942), the author of the "Anne of Green Gables" books, was a most sensitive and highly imaginative woman. She was raised in the vicinity of the village of Cavendish, P.E.I. Throughout her life she held the farming region of her native island province in high regard for its beauty and its evocative qualities. These two passages evoke an atmosphere suitable for ghost stories, both real and imagined. They come from her private writings which have been collected in The Selected Journals of L.M. Montgomery: Volume I: 1889-1910 *(Toronto: Oxford University Press, 1985), edited by Mary Rubio and Elizabeth Waterston.*

Monday, Nov. 18, 1907
Cavendish, P.E.I.

I HAD A WALK through Lover's Lane at dark tonight — or just as the dark was coming down. I was never there so late before and while I enjoyed it I was really a little bit afraid, with a not unpleasant fear. The whole character of the lane seemed changed. It was mysterious, sibilant, remote, eerie. The trees, my old well-known friends, were strange and aloof. The sounds I heard were not the cheery, companionable chorus of daytime — they were creeping and whispering and weird, as if the life of the woods had suddenly developed something almost hostile — at least alien and unacquainted and furtive. I could have fancied that I heard stealthy footsteps all around me and I felt the old, primitive unreasoning fear that was known to the childhood of the race — the awe of the dark and the shadowy, the shrinking from some unseen danger lurking in the gloom. My twentieth-century reason quelled it into a rather piquant watchfulness — but it would not have taken much to deliver me over to a blind panic in which I would have turned and fled shamelessly. As it was, when I left the lane I walked more quickly than my wont and felt as if I had escaped from some fascinating but not altogether hallowed locality — a place still given over to paganism and the revels of fauns and satyrs. None of the wild places are ever wholly Christianized in the darkness, however much so they may seem by daylight. There is always a lurking life in them that dare not show itself to the sun but regains its own with the night.

Sunday, Dec. 14, 1907
Cavendish, P.E.I.

To-night I did something which twenty years ago I could never have imagined myself doing. What was this startling thing? Why, I walked *alone* through the "Cavendish Road woods" *after dark*.

When I was a child I had the greatest horror of those woods. A mile in along the road lived a family of "Jacks," who kept a small — a very small — shop where they sold tea, sugar, etc. I was frequently sent in to buy some houeshold supplies and I shall *never* forget the agony of terror I used to endure going along that wooded road. The distance through the woods was not more than a quarter of a mile but it seemed endless to me. I never dared tell anyone of my terror for I would have been laughed at and ridicule was even more dreadful to me than the nameless horrors that lay in wait for me in those woods. I cannot define just what I was afraid of — I could not have put my dread into words. It was just the old primitive fear handed down to us from ancestors in the dawn of time who were afraid of the woods with good reason. It was on my part just a blind, unreasoning terror. But this was all in the daylight. To go through those woods *after dark* was simply not to be contemplated. I could not understand how anyone *could* do it. I remember a young schoolteacher who boarded here and who used to go in there at night to transact school business with a trustee who lived on the other side. In my eyes he was the greatest hero the world has ever seen.

But tonight I came through them. I don't remember ever coming through them after dark *alone* before. They are out of the way of my twilight peregrinations and I've always had company on that road. But I was alone tonight and I liked it. I never even remembered that I used to be frightened of those woods long ago until I came home. I don't feel at all heroic.

I wonder if all the things we look forward to with dread in the future will not be like this. When we come to them we shall not mind them — we shall not be afraid.

2. Ghosts Have Warm Hands

Will R. Bird

Will R. Bird (1891-1984), one of Nova Scotia's best-
loved sons, wrote twenty-seven books, many of them historical
romances. The most notable among them, Here Stays Good Yorkshire
(1945), recreates the life of Yorkshire settlers in the Chignecto region at
the time of the American Revolution. Sunrise for Peter and Other
Stories (1946) is a fine collection of short fiction.

Bird is also the author of two memoirs, And We Go On (1930) and
Ghosts Have Warm Hands (1968). The latter book deals with his
experiences during the First World War, when he served with the 42nd
Royal Highlanders of Canada. The following excerpt from that book
describes part of Bird's service in France, including participation in the
brilliant assault on Vimy Ridge, Easter Monday, 9 April 1917. A short
while thereafter he encountered the ghost of his dead brother.

WE LEFT THE RIDGE and went to Vimy village, relieving C.M.R.'s
(Canadian Mounted Rifles) there, and doing working parties, digging
trenches, putting up wire near the front line. During the first night I
was sent out with two men as a covering party for the men working
with the barbed wire. It was cold and miserable. We were made to
inspect the area through binoculars so we would recognize the various
landmarks and not put the wire in a wrong place. We were out soon
after it was dark but did not take nearly enough wire the first time and
had to return for more. So it was midnight before we were finished.

Luckily the Hun did not hear anything, but it was very chilling to stay crouched in position for hours, and the night seemed endless. All I could think of was the fact I had no place to go when we were through. Getting our party ready had taken so long that I had had no chance to prepare any sort of shelter.

As we went back and drew near the railway embankment someone called in a low voice. I went over and found two of the men from the 73rd had dug a neat bivvy into the embankment. They were very decent chaps and insisted they had made the place wide enough to accommodate the three of us. We snuggled in, and with a ground sheet pegged to hold over our heads we were really comfortable. In seconds I was dead to the world.

The ground sheet pegged over our heads was pulled free and fell on my face, rousing me. Then a firm hand seized one of mine and pulled me up to a sitting position. It was very early, as first sunshine was glittering on the dew-wet grass. I was annoyed that I should have to do some chore after being out so late. I tried to pull free. But the grip held, and as I came to a sitting-up position my other hand was seized and I had a look at my visitor.

In an instant I was out of the bivvy, so surprised I could not speak. I was face to face with my brother, Steve, who had been killed in '15!

The first notice form the War Office had said: "Missing, believed dead." After a time one of his mates wrote to say a boot had been found with his name on it. The Germans had mined the Canadian trench and blown it up.

Steve grinned as he released my hands, then put his warm hand over my mouth as I started to shout my happiness. He pointed to the sleepers in the bivvy and to my rifle and equipment. "Get your gear," he said softly.

As I grabbed it he turned and started walking away rapidly. It was hard to keep up with him. We passed make-shift shelters filled with sleeping men of my platoon. No one was awake. Now and then a gun fired off toward the Somme or a machine-gun chattered, but on the whole it was a quiet morning. As soon as we were past the shelters I hurried to get close to Steve. "Why didn't you write Mother?" I asked.

He turned and the grin was still on his face. "Wait," he said. "Don't talk yet."

Then I noticed he had a soft cap on and no gas mask or equipment.

Somehow he had learned where the 42nd was, and our "D" Company, but how in the world did he know where I was sleeping?

We left the company area and headed directly into a collection of ruins that had been Petit Vimy. "There's no one around here," I said. "How did you know where to find me?"

At that moment my equipment, slung hurried over one shoulder, slipped off and fell to the ground before I could catch it. As I stooped and retrieved it Steve went into a passageway in the ruins and I ran to catch him. Arrived there, I saw one way went right and the other left. Which way had he gone? "Steve!" I called. There was no answer, so I dropped my rifle and gear and ran to the right. It only took minutes — two or three — to get to the far side, but there was no sign of my brother. I ran back and called again, took the way to the left, searched and searched again, called repeatedly, but could not find him. Finally I sat down on my equipment and leaned back against a bit of wall. I was tired and sweating and excited. A great desire to find our officer and get the day off took hold of me, but I realized I did not know where the officer or sergeant-major were, and if I left the immediate area and Steve returned he would not know where I had gone. Probably he had no pass and did not want to be seen. If only I had not bothered with my equipment I could have kept up with him!

Minutes went by. I got up and made another search of the ruins. The sun began to glisten on the tops of the broken walls. I settled back more comfortably on my equipment and heard the usual morning stir of guns firing registering shots. The sun got warmer. I dozed.

Suddenly I was shaken awake. Tommy had me by the arm and was yelling, "He's here! Bill's here!"

I stumbled up, dazed, looked at my watch. It was nine o'clock.

"What's made you come here?" Tommy was asking.

"What happened?"

"You should know. They're digging around the bivvy you were in. All they've found is Jim's helmet and one of Bob's legs."

"Legs!" I echoed stupidly. "What do you mean?"

"Don't you know a big shell landed in that bivvy? They've been trying to find something of you."

It seemed utterly incredible. I put on my gear and followed Tommy. There was a great cavity in the embankment and debris was scattered over the whole area. Mickey came running to shake hands with me.

Then the sergeant was calling and I saw he was talking with an officer.

When we got nearer I saw it was an artillery officer of high rank and saluted him.

"What made you leave the bivvy?" the sergeant asked. "The boys say you got in there with Jim and Bob."

"I did," I said. "I was there till daylight."

"What made you leave then?"

It was the artillery officer who asked the question, and I hesitated, felt it would sound foolish if I told them exactly what had happened.

"Don't be afraid," he said. "We're all friends."

He looked a real gentleman, so I told him my story in detail. He made notes in a book he carried, asking my name, where I was from, and all about Steve. Then he shook my hand. "You have had a wonderful experience," he said.

The sergeant looked as if he did not know whether to believe me or not, but a runner came with orders for another move and I hustled to get something to eat. Neither Tommy nor Mickey mentioned the matter to me through the day, and that night we were over to the left doing working parties again until late. I slept in a bivvy MacDonald and I had made but it was past midnight before I could doze off.

I had seen Steve as clearly as I saw Mickey. His warm hands had pulled me from the bivvy. His voice had been perfectly natural. He had the old half-grin I knew so well. He had saved my life.

I had joined the Methodist Church when I was fourteen and had been as decent as the average. At evenings in the Y.M.C.A. I loved the singing of hymns. I did not like the compulsory church service and the officers singing "O God, Our Help in Ages Past." But now I knew beyond all argument or theory, by any man learned or otherwise, that there was a hereafter, and there would never again be the slightest doubt in my mind about it.

For a few days I sensed that the sergeant had not believed my story but it did not worry me in the least. Then a batman let me know the officers had talked about the incident and regarded my story as the result of too much rum. This was rather amusing as I never took the ration and everyone in our company, except the officers who were new, was aware of the fact. However, in a few days the matter was forgotten by the men. And it was only as I lay ready for sleep that I thought of it.

Everywhere I Go I See Ghosts

Michael J. Bakerpearce

The correspondent who wrote this interesting letter lives in Damascus — not the Damascus of the Middle East, however, but the Damascus in Ontario, the one located near Kenilworth.

Michael J. Bakerpearce's background is English, with Welsh and Irish ancestors. He was born in a hamlet called Cowers Lane, not far from Derby, England. He immigrated to Canada and from 1969 until 1987, when he took early retirement, he worked in the University of Guelph's Department of Pathology as a histology technologist.

If you ask Mr. Bakerpearce the question, "Are some people naturally psychic?" you may be sure that his answer will be a resounding "Yes!"

Damascus, Ont.
Wednesday, 13 June 1990.

DEAR MR. COLOMBO,

I read in the *Guelph Mercury* that you are interested in "people who have extraordinary experiences."

I suppose I am one of those people, my friends and family tell me so, but to me those experiences do not seem extraordinary. You see, apart from other things, I see ghosts. I have always "seen" them, as long as I can remember. As a child I used to think everyone saw them, alas! I used to get into trouble, as no doubt you can imagine. People don't like people who are "different" — especially if they are small children.

I am what people call "psychic." I don't like the word myself as I don't think it describes properly the phenomenon, but I think "clairvoyant" is a bit pompous. I was always thus, and I used to take a lot of abuse and ridicule because of it, until I learned to keep my mouth shut. But, of course, if one has to suppress things psychic, they tend to atrophy from misuse, or unuse, like muscles and memory.

The worst problem I had was as a small child, just over four years. It was in England, 1929, my oldest uncle (sixty years then) was about to emigrate to Canada. The kitchen was full of people, and the Immigration Officer was there too, and he was trying to talk my dad into coming to Canada because we were a big family (seven and another on the way). But Dad only had one arm, and no real trade; he'd lost an arm in WW1 and all he knew was soldiering and gymnastics, and he was afraid to commit himself and his family to a hard life in Canada.

Anyway, in the heat of the discussion, I went to Uncle Jack and said something. The next thing I knew was my mum bending over me giving me such a tongue-lashing and telling me to stop telling fortunes. I never could remember what I had said, and she would never tell me.

However, my oldest brother ran away just before WW2. We heard nothing from him until the mid-1980s, when he rejoined what was left of the family. He had changed his name and settled in Canada after WW2. So it was that I met him again after forty-seven years. He had never tried to contact the family until that time, and knew nothing of what might have happened to his parents, nor to any of his brothers or sisters.

In the course of some reminiscing, I asked him if he remembered the incident and what I had said that had made Mum so angry. He told me what I had said.

It seems I went to Uncle Jack and, right in one of those awful lulls that come in conversations among a crowd of people, said in a clear, loud voice, "It's no use you going to Canada, Uncle Jack — you'll be dead in two years." As my brother said, "All the family knew you were clairvoyant, so you can understand the trouble it caused."

Well, Uncle Jack and his family came to Canada in the spring of 1930. I did not come until twenty-five years later. By this time Uncle Jack had died, leaving a widow and two children, the ones he had left with.

In 1957, I drove, with my wife, down to New Brunswick to meet my aunt and her family. While we were there, my aunt asked me if I would like to see where Jack was buried, so we went to the little graveyard and looked at his little headstone. It said: "John C. / Born 1870. Died 1932."

I remember I said to my aunt, "So he died just two years after leaving England, eh?" And she said, "Yes. You see, you were right, after all." Something happened to distract us and I didn't ask her to explain what she had said, but I never could understand why she said it; that is, until my oldest brother told me the story. I'm told that sort of thing is an "extraordinary experience," although I do not find it so.

I see ghosts. Everywhere I go I see ghosts. I used to think everyone did. How do you prove you see ghosts? Do you have to? I could fill books with ghost stories: the time I saw Mary Queen of Scots at Winfield Manor, and again at Tutbury Castle; the day I stood in the entrance to Westminster Abbey and saw the whole ceremony of the burial of the Unknown Soldier in 1919, in colour, and smelt the ladies' perfume and the horses' sweat, and heard the guns firing; when I told my mother about it she said, "You must have seen it in a film." I had to remind her that any film of the ceremony would have been in black and white.

Then there was the time, more recently, when my mother-in-law paid me a visit the very moment she died, to make amends for the trouble she thought she had caused when my wife and I came to Canada.

Often I used to see my father, only with two arms instead of one — and so on and so on.

Then there's the time I went "astrally" (a silly name) to visit a friend's apartment, and described it to her exactly the next day. Another young woman said she didn't believe it unless I could do the same for her. I told her she would have to leave her apartment, and she agreed, but when I "arrived" she was lying naked on her bed waiting for me. I even saw the dark mole on her left breast. When I spoke to her about it the next day, I knew she had seen me. All the other folk who were interested in what I was doing knew what had gone on without my having to tell them.

Then there was the time that my oldest brother was in hospital, dying of lung cancer, and I "went" to see him and described the room to my niece the next day on the phone; however, the next night when I "went," they had moved him down the corridor to another room, but I was able to describe the decor of that room too.

But how can I prove any of this?

Ian Currie, the author of *You Cannot Die*, whom I knew at the University of Guelph, asked me how I managed to live in two worlds, the world of the living and the world of the dead. I told him I lived in one world: a world peopled with the living and the dead. He said he had never thought of it that way before.

Anyway, I'd better quit, or I'll not get any of my "work" done. I am retired, but busier than I was when I worked.

I'll pass the Crystal Ball to you, and I hope to hear from you soon.

Sincerely,
Michael J. Bakerpearce

4. We Had to Creep Past

Anna D. M. Bill

*A*nna D.M. Bill, *a resident of Puslinch, Ontairo, responded to my letter requesting "ghost stories" which appeared in* The Guelph Daily Mercury.

Here is part of Mrs. Bill's letter of 24 May 1990. It deals with an experience that took place in Germany in the 1930s. It is interesting to note how vividly a scary experience of this sort stands out in memory, and how it becomes a permament part of one's life.

ABOUT SIXTY YEARS AGO my brother (then aged about eleven) and I were walking a back street in the medieval town of Marburg/Lahn, Germany. It was just after Christmas. We wanted to look at the Christmas trees in peoples' living-rooms. The windows were at street level and overlooked the back alley. Nobody drew their curtains because nobody ever walked there at night. Snow was all around.

Just as we neared a conjunction of little alleys, out of the ground, with a horrible shriek, there rose a figure in medieval, glowing armour. We withdrew into the doorway of a metre-thick wall, petrified.

How long we stayed there I can't remember, but we were getting very cold. At last we decided to make a dash for it, but we had to creep past this apparition for we were afraid to go the long way back.

As we passed him, he shrieked again. Then we ran. He followed us. Then we shrieked. Neighbours looked out of their windows. My parents and grandmother came outside to see what was the matter.

I had fallen flat on my face. My brother had lost his brand-new sailor cap, a Christmas present. There was absolutely no traffic at that time and place, just pure, clean snow and a dim streetlamp. The apparition continued on to the ancient churchyard cemetery.

The sailor cap was never found. The site of the cemetery is now a school playground.

Neither of us has ever forgotten the slightest detail of this experience, despite the passage of years.

5. Weird and Strange Happenings

Rex Loring

Millions of CBC Radio listeners across the country regard Rex Loring as a personal friend. The radio announcer has a distinctive name, a voice that is smooth and soothing, and an authoritative manner of speaking. It was a national news story in 1990 when this English-born veteran broadcaster retired from the Corporation after many years of service.

Parapsychologists employ the Greek letter psi to designate possible psychic power or ability. The four manifestations of psi are considered to be telepathy (the power of mind reading), clairvoyance (knowledge at a distance), precognition (knowledge of the future), and psychokinesis (the power of the unaided mind over matter).

"Psi among Canadians" was the subject of a series of radio programs broadcast on the CBC's Trans-Canada Network between July and September 1962. CBC producers invited men and women from all walks of life to send accounts of their psychical and paranormal experiences. Over three hundred letters were received, and these were examined for recurring patterns by J. B. Rhine and J. G. Pratt, noted psychologists with the Parapsychology Laboratory at Duke University in Durham, North Carolina.

Rex Loring submitted an experience of his own. The experience was based on memories of his childhood in England. The account *was broadcast by CBC Radio and then published by magazine writer and editor Sidney Katz in* Maclean's *in its issue of 29 July 1961.*

I'M NO AUTHORITY on weird and strange happenings. I'm not even particularly interested in them. But I can clearly recall two experiences I had, when I was living with my grandmother as a boy that still baffle me.

At two o'clock one morning half a dozen plates went hurtling down from a shelf and smashed into small pieces on the floor. There was no reason for this to have happened. There were no earth tremors and the plates were firmly held in place by a string of moulding. My grandmother awoke and promptly announced, "I must dress and go to Mother's house. She has just died." She was right.

The plates were replaced by new ones. About six months later, again in the middle of the night, they went flying to the floor and broke into smithereens. This time my grandmother said, "My sister has just passed away." Again, she was right.

Incidents such as these, I'm told, are caused by poltergeists — noisy ghosts or spirits that make their presence felt by knocking or throwing things around. Were the plates, on these two occasions, moved by the spirits of Grandmother's mother and sister? I don't know. I do know that the plates did fall for no apparent reason.

6. But No One Would Be There

R.M.Y.

About five miles outside the city of Bathurst, New Brunswick, there is a farmhouse that is held to be haunted. Members of the family who live there report hearing strange sounds — footsteps when no one else is around. It is said that the farmhouse stands close to the foundations of an old log cabin which local residents considered to be haunted. Anyway, family members who live in the farmhouse continue to report hearing those footsteps.

The full name of the narrator of the following account of the haunting is not known, but her initials are preserved: R.M.Y. Her account was written in response to a request for such experiences carried by local newspapers. The request was made by Winifred G. Barton and published in her book Psychic Phenomena in Canada *(Ottawa: Psi-Science Productions Ltd., c. 1967).*

I THOUGHT YOU MIGHT BE INTERESTED in my experience of a few years ago. Up until that time I never believed in the supernatural. I was born in London, England, and came to Canada with my family when I was five years old. At the time of this incident I was a married woman with a family.

We moved into a new house about five miles from Bathurst in 1935. Some of the neighbours told me that it was built a few feet from where an old log cabin had been torn down. The cabin was supposedly haunted and the local people were scared to pass by after dark. But I am not a nervous person and considered these stories quite ridiculous. I never did bother to enquire what form the haunting took.

In October 1936 my parents came down for a visit. The next morning I awoke early and lay waiting for the alarm clock to signal time to get up when I heard footsteps going downstairs. Thinking it was my mother I hurried down to send her back to bed, but when I passed her room I saw her still sleeping. On going downstairs I had the distinct feeling that I was not alone. I looked around but no one was there, and as all the doors were locked from the inside, no one could have gone out.

On the following day I awakened just in time to start down to kindle the fire. Mother was awake so as I passed her room I stopped to talk with her for a minute. She asked where I was going. I said I was about to light the kitchen fire. Mother looked surprised and said: "But you just came up. I heard you coming and saw you pass the door. At least I saw a form I took to be you. I wondered why you didn't speak to me...."

For a couple of years nothing unusual happened. Then, during the winter of 1939-40, on several occasions when I was sitting in the living room, listening to the radio about 9:30 p.m., I would hear the sound of the back door opening and shutting, then the shuffle of a few quiet footsteps. At first I thought this was my husband returning from the Armouries and walking over to the kitchen table to put his lunch box down. When he didn't speak and all was silent I would investigate. But no one would be there. My husband coming in a little later would deny having been in the house earlier.

I was the only one who heard these noises until one evening when my fourteen-year-old son stayed up to speak to his father; we both heard the sounds at the same time. He described it exactly as I had heard it.

On another occasion my husband was home when it happened. He said: "You'd better put the light on in the kitchen. Someone just came in...." I was so relieved that he heard the noises too, for I was starting to think there might be something wrong with me. They were so normal in every respect that I never failed to go and see who had come in.

Our dog, an excellent watchdog who heard the slightest sound on the door, never seemed to notice a thing — any other sound and he would bark his head off!

7. I Awakened with a Jump

F. D. Blackley

"*An Early Morning Visitor to the Abandoned Hotel*" *is the title that was given to this narrative when it made its first appearance on a page headed "Ghost Stories" published in the* Edmonton Journal *on 30 Oct. 1988. The author of the story is F.D. Blackley, a resident of Edmonton, who describes a scary episode in his life as a student in Southern Ontario in the late 1930s.*

IN THE SUMMER before the outbreak of the Second World War, my girlfriend had a summer job in a small town on Lake Ontario.

One afternoon I hitchhiked from Toronto to see her. We had a pleasant evening, including a walk along the beach. I noticed an abandoned building, presumably an old hotel, a little distance from the water, in a grove of trees. Eventually, I parted with the young lady and had to decide what I should do for the night, as it was now dark.

A university student, I had very little money. I considered the town hotel but it was very close to the chiming town clock, which I knew would bother me. I recalled the abandoned building and thought that I might find a dry spot there on which to curl up until morning.

I went back to the beach and had no problem entering the

building. I went to the second floor. This had a long, central hall with many rooms opening from it on either side. I took a room at the far end of the hall with a window that overlooked the roof of a porch. I lay down on a raincoat that I had brought with me.

About 4:00 a.m., while it was still dark, I awakened with a jump. It was as if I had been startled by a loud noise, although I am convinced that this had not been so. I stood up and looked down the hall, lit by a bit of moonlight from a window over the stair. Coming towards me was an indistinct figure with a softly burning lantern.

It was entering each room in turn as if it were looking for someone or something. As it neared my end of the hall, I saw its face, a horrible one that seemed to drip evil. Worse, perhaps, I could see some of the details of the hall through its body. I did not wait for the lantern-carrier to enter my room. I went out the window onto the porch roof. As I jumped to the ground, I could see the lantern flashing in my "bedroom."

I went uptown and found an all-night truck stop where I had coffee to calm my nerves, and some breakfast. The cafe wasn't very busy and I was able to ask the proprietor about the abandoned building by the beach. It had been a hotel, he said, but it had not been successful. Some locals, he added, said that it was haunted by an old man with a lantern! He didn't believe the story. I did not tell him that I did.

8. The Apparition Experience

William D'Arcy Lennie

Ed Needham is the host of a popular phone-in program on CFRB Radio in Toronto. Ed is an interesting guy, the spitting image of the actor Leslie Nielsen, so I felt I was "among the stars" when Ed invited me to be a guest on his early evening show on 6 Nov. 1988. The topic of our discussion was paranormal experiences.

During our ninety-minute conversation, which was full of delightful digressions, we heard from more than a dozen callers. Almost all of them sounded sincere; a couple of them sounded troubled as they recounted experiences that seemed inexplicable. Ed and I were quite impressed with the quality of the contributions of a number of the callers. We found the apparition experience told by one of the callers, whose name we then did not know, to be particularly interesting. The story he concisely recalled is almost classic in its configuration.

I suggested that the caller might care to leave his name and phone number with the program's producer when he went off the air. He did this, and two days later I talked with the caller, William D'Arcy Lennie, and he agreed to share his experience and some biographical particulars with my readers. Mr. Lennie was born in 1924. During the Second World War he served with the RCAF in Canada and England as an Air Gunnery Instructor. For some years he *operated his own personnel consultant business in Toronto. He is currently a part-time, client-service representative for a leading trust company.*

AS REQUESTED, in our telephone conversation of December 8th, I am pleased to describe the apparition experience.

I lived in Hamilton, Ontario, with my parents from 1930 to 1937. In August of 1936, we were asked down for a long weekend to a cottage on Lake Erie that an uncle and aunt, Mr. and Mrs. H.K. Hunt, had rented. We drove down from Hamilton, and I sat in the back seat of the car with my head between my father and mother. The land was quite flat with no ditches on either side. I noticed a farm house with a high hedge around it on my right side.

As we approached the farm house I saw a tall man dressed in a suit and fedora come out of the hedge. On seeing him I felt a cold chill run down my back. It felt like ice water. My mother screamed at my father to stop the car or he'd kill the man. The man never turned his head, but proceeded across the road, walking and yet not walking; you could say, "semi-floating." On reaching the other side of the road, the apparition vanished.

The three of us got out of the car and there was nothing — absolutely no cover or place you could hide in — a completely flat area with no trees or bushes. The time of day was about 5:00 p.m.

On reaching the cottage we found my aunt and uncle were entertaining a couple who lived in the adjoining cottage. My father told everyone about our experience. My uncle and aunt were very sceptical and laughed. The couple who lived next door didn't say a word. Uncle Harry asked them if the story wasn't a little far-fetched. The neighbour, who had been a cottage-owner for years, said, "No, it isn't far-fetched. A year ago to the day, and at almost the exact time, a man was killed in front of that farm house by a car."

My father, mother, and I had no prior knowledge of the car fatality.

Please do not hesitate to contact me if you have any further questions.

9. I Couldn't Exactly See Him

Helen Brens

Helen Brens, a design draftswoman, described the following experience. It occurred to her in Montreal at some point during the Second World War. What she saw, or otherwise experienced, was not the ghost of a dead person but the apparation of someone who was living. Maclean's published her experience in a special feature devoted to "Psi in Canada" in its issue of 29 July 1961.

I RETURNED HOME after being out one night. I didn't bother switching on the lights. I could walk up the stairs, which are in the dining-room, to my bedroom in the dark. Suddenly I became aware that someone was standing against the wall at the foot of the stairs. I couldn't actually see him but I was certain of it.

I wasn't too frightened. I was certain it must have been Dad who had got up to check on the front door and, hearing me come, decided he was going to have some fun and scare me for wandering around in the dark. I remember, as I started up the stairs, I moved over to one side to avoid bumping into him. But when I reched the exact spot I realized that there was nobody there. Dad was asleep in bed. For some reason the joy and excitement vanished suddenly.

Some years after, a friend of mine who is a sea captain came to visit me. He told me that his ship had been torpedoed. He and fifteen of his men managed to get on a raft. After several days there were only three survivors left, including my friend. The rest had become exhausted and were swept into the sea. I asked my friend what he thought about during the final hours before his rescue.

"One of my most comforting thoughts," he said, "was imagining myself standing in your dining room at the foot of your dining-room stairs watching you and your family go through the daily routine of living."

As nearly as I could make out, he was on the raft at the time my experience took place.

I ask you — was it a trick of the imagination or was there someone standing at the foot of the stairs that night?

10. *That Light that Night Saved His Life*

Mary O'Donnell

O*n 7 March 1989, I was the guest of David Carr on his open-line show on radio station CFOS in Owen Sound, Ontario. We talked for ninety minutes on psychical and other matters, and we listened as callers shared their paranormal experiences with us and the show's listeners.*

One of the listeners was Mary O'Donnell of Port Elgin who, later that day, wrote out an account of her own experience and sent it to me. In her letter she recalled a Lindsay family tradition of a forerunner, a forewarning of death....

March 7, 1989

DEAR MR. COLOMBO:

This morning I listened to the radio programme from Owen Sound and found it fascinating. I'd like to tell you something that happened in our family, the Lindsay family, a long time ago (in the 1940s).

My grandmother was dying, and all the members of her family had come to our house in Timmins where she stayed. They had been there a few weeks when my Uncle Len, who worked on the railway out of North Bay, decided that he would return to work the next day.

That night a strange light played up and down the door of my grandmother's bedroom. It was like the headlight of a train engine.

I was not there at the time but later, when I came home, I heard them all talking about it. They all believed it was a sign that my grandmother would die the next day. They felt that my Uncle Len should not return to North Bay the next day but should remain in Timmins for the funeral.

Well, Grandmother did not die the next day, but she did die a few days later. Uncle Len remained in Timmins, and it is a good thing that he did. If he had returned to North Bay, as planned, he would have joined one of two crews that worked out of North Bay. All the men on those crews were killed in a head-on collision east of North Bay. I believe the crash took place at Rutherglen.

When we took Grandmother's body by train for burial in Mattawa, we passed the scene of the crash. The engines were lying down the slope and were still smoking.

My Uncle Len lived for many years after that, but I'm sure of one thing: That light that night saved his life.

I hope you find this interesting.

Sincerely,
(Mrs.) Mary O'Donnell

11. I Had Had the Strangest Feeling

Florence Liddell

*A*udiences in Canada, like audiences around the world, were thrilled by the theme and excitement of the film Chariots of Fire. *This fine motion picture, released in the fall of 1977, told the true story of the conflict that occurred when a man was forced to measure the worth of friendship, weigh the value of religious principle, and make a considerable sacrifice to reconcile them.*

Chariots of Fire *is based on the rivalry between two British university students, one a Scottish Congregational Christian, the other an English Reform Jew. As young athletes they were magnificent sprinters who vied for Olympic honours.*

In the movie the part of Eric Liddell was played to perfection by Ian Charleson. On the screen, as in life, Liddell devoted his adult life to his work as a missionary in China. He died in a Japanese internment camp at Weihsien on 21 Feb. 1945.

It is of particular Canadian interest that one of the influences on Liddell's life was that of his wife. She was born Florence McKenzie, the daughter of Canadian Christian missionaries who were based in Toronto. Florence trained in that city as a nurse and, like her parents, dedicated her life to missioning in China.

Liddell had met Florence's parents in China. He visited the family in Toronto on a number of occasions and the local press interviewed him as "Scotland's greatest athlete."

The couple were married at Tientsin in China in 1934. They had three daughters, Patricia, Heather, and Maureen.

Liddell was caught in China during the Second World War. Florence and their daughters spent the war years in Toronto, where she was informed that her husband had died some two months earlier. How she learned of Eric's death is recorded in her own words in The Flying Scotsman *(London: Quartet Books, 1981) by Sally Magnusson. It seems that Florence was visited by Eric's spirit.*

Magnusson began the account of how Florence learned of his death with these words: "On 2 May 1945, more than two months after Eric's death, two family friends arrived at the house where Florence Liddell was staying in Toronto, her parents' home. They asked if her mother were in."

I INVITED THEM IN and I sensed there was something wrong. So finally I said to them, "Have you got bad news? Is it one of the boys?" (I had two brothers, you know.) Even then it never crossed my mind that it would be Eric.

About a month before this visit, I had had the strangest feeling. I was standing at the stove and I thought, "If you turn round, Eric is standing there." I could just feel vibrations. He was so full of life and bouncy. And he said, "It's OK, Flossie. Everything is going to be all right." (Flossie is the name he always used to tease me; it used to make me mad!) I thought my nerves were going. For three weeks I was conscious of his presence in this way. But it never crossed my mind that he had died. I am sure that somehow or other he was allowed to come back.

I was terribly crushed when I got the news. I was all for jumping off the bridge. But again his influence was just *there*; as if he were saying, "Florence, what are you going to accomplish by jumping off the bridge?" I was thinking I would catch up with Eric that way, but he would just look at me as if to say, "Flo, what about the three little girls I've left in your care?" And that stopped me.

I had had no hint that he was even ill. Three or four Red Cross letters from him came after I heard he was dead, and one mentioned that he was in hospital and that they thought he might be working too hard. He got these terrible headaches at that time and he got depressed because he had always thought his faith would carry him through. A couple from the Salvation Army wrote to me afterwards and said they had seen him putting his hand to the wall to steady himself sometimes. That's when I really felt bad.

He had told me nothing about what life was like in the camp. He just talked about the children and said he was helping with the sports. They had to be very circumspect in their letters. Generally, on the back of the letter form there was a space where you could reply; and it would take from six months to a year for a letter to go back and forwards.

Eric was ten years older than me, you know. I'd like to have seen what he looked like today. He was eternally young — even though he had very little hair. He used to make jokes about it, but his mother was very perturbed and swore it was because he took too many showers.

I liked the way they portrayed him in the film — *Chariots of Fire*, is that its name? It was just exactly Eric. It moved me very much. I especially liked the way they had him in Paris telling the Prince of Wales he would not run on a Sunday. The way he was so quiet but stood up for himself and firmly answered back.

He certainly threw himself into his running, didn't he? The way he threw his head back — it was so ridiculous! Boy, I couldn't understand how he could even see. When I ever asked him he just said, "I knew where I was going all right." He had the most beautiful laugh.

12. The Spirit of Karinthy

George Faludy

George Faludy, the distinguished Hungarian poet and man-of-letters, in the account that follows, pays tribute to an earlier distinguished Hungarian poet and man-of-letters named Frederic Karinthy — whose spirit lives on in the world of Hungarian literature if not in the netherworld of the afterworld.

Faludy, as a leading emigré writer, lived in Toronto from 1968 to 1989 and acquired Canadian citizenship. His recent publications in English include Selected Poems, translated by Robin Skelton, and Notes from the Rain Forest, written in English with the assistance of Eric Johnson.

The following account comes from a letter which Faludy posted to the present editor in October 1989. The envelope bears a Budapest postmark. Following the easing of relations between the communist and capitalist empires, Faludy returned to his native Hungary to considerable acclaim. He now finds that his books, once outlawed but not forgotten, are being reprinted. It seems the prophet is with honour in his own country....

FREDERIC KARINTHY (1887-1938) was a very fine and singularly gifted Hungarian writer; I find no one in the body of literature of the West (or of the East for that matter) with whom to compare him, if only to characterize him and his writings. He was a satirist, in the sense of Swift; he was the writer of light sketches which still prove, after eighty years, to be true to life; he was, on occasion, a poet of high seriousness. He greeted the Nazi movement with a little verse which concluded: "I prefer that all the little vermin swallow me up than that I swallow up all the little vermin." Everything considered, he was a genius — the sort of genius someone at the age of sixteen imagines a genius to be: hundred-sided, interested in everything, magnanimous, amusing. Each year he recorded hundreds of his ideas in that year's notebook. He employed dozens of these ideas in his writings, and then, every January the first, he discarded the notebook, maintaining that there was no need to carry the old ideas with him into the new year. Knowing everyone and everything, he was still an utter stranger to this world. At night, standing helplessly before the gate to the house where he had just rung the bell, he looked like an alien being who had, just five minutes earlier, been dropped by parachute from some distant star-world onto our planet.

I knew him from those literary coffee-houses in Budapest where he was wont to spend most of his days, and from the literary salon of Dr. Totis, where writers, actors, and artists met most evenings. Karinthy was not a spiritualist, but once at Dr. Totis's house he remarked, loud enough for everyone to hear, that should his soul survive the final dissolution of his body — a prospect that he admitted he found highly unlikely — he would try to communicate with us. He would do so just as, seven hundred years earlier, Averroes, the Arab philosopher, communicated with the Jewish doctor Ben Jussef in Cordova. (I once read about this incident in Ernest Renan's book *Averroes*.) I do not now remember whether it was Ben Jussef or Averroes who was the first to die. But, early one morning, the survivor was roused from his sleep by the sight and sound of the dead one riding over a cobblestoned street in Cordova, with great laughter and the words: "Everything is different!" While still alive, they had made a pact that the first to die would inform the other of the event and of the survival of the soul (although Averroes maintained the following: "God would not have created us mortal had he intended to recreate us immortal.").

Karinthy's death occurred in 1938 at the time of the Munich agreement. Exactly one year later, Totis, as a Jewish doctor of leftist convictions who was much hated by the Hungarian government, the right wing of which was then in power, was living with his wife as an immigrant in Paris. So was I. We had long forgotten the story about Averroes and Ben Jussef; we were soon reminded of it. However, we did not forget Karinthy. One year to the day of his death, I and a few friends were invited to Totis's shabby hotel room to recall Karinthy with a bottle of cheap red wine — *vin ordinaire*, as the French call it.

There was a power blackout. The room had two beds, side by side, with a couch across the foot of the beds. We sat on the couch, on the floor before the couch, and on the two chairs on the side of the couch. With regard to the power blackout, which the authorities were taking very seriously, only the bedside table-lamp was burning. It was nine or ten feet away from us. As we spoke about Karinthy, the table-lamp blinked and then went out. "Power failure," we said. But a few seconds later, the lamp went on. We continued to talk. The lamp blinked again and went out. "Karinthy!" somebody said. "Bullshit!" we all added. After a similar short interval of darkness, the lamp went on again. Then, after a similar interval, the lamp blinked for the third time, went out again, and went on again — it seemed after intervals that were similar to the previous ones. We were all surprised and impressed. That is the reason I never forgot the story of Averroes and the Jewish doctor Ben Jussef of Cordova.

After the fall of France, Dr. Totis and his wife returned to Hungary where they were brutally murdered by the Nazis. My friend Andrew Havas, also present on the occasion, was murdered by his fellow Communists. Now I no longer remember who else was present to witness the curious incident.

13. Content to Accept It as Inexplicable

George Woodcock

*I*t might be said that Canadian literature came of age *when George Woodcock, the distinguished man-of-letters, returned to Canada and some years later was appointed the founding editor of the quarterly journal* Canadian Literature. *Its first issue appeared in the fall of 1959.*

Woodock was born in Winnipeg but he lived in England and worked for many years in literary circles in London where he befriended many well-known British writers, including George Orwell. Following his return to Canada, he befriended many of this country's leading writers. Anecdotes about them brighten the pages of Woodcock's two highly readable volumes of memoirs, Letter to the Past: An Autobiography *(1982) and* Beyond the Blue Mountains *(1987), both published in Toronto by Fitzhenry & Whiteside.*

The Woodcocks are no strangers to "the mysterious," as these five vividly written excerpts from the two books attest. (The first and second sections come from Letter to the Past; *the third, fourth, and fifth from* Beyond the Blue Mountain).

The first excerpt recounts some events surrounding the departure of the Woodcocks for Canada from England in 1949. One event was the premonition, experienced by George, that Marie Louise, a close friend from his anarchist days, had died.

The second excerpt finds the Woodcocks in Vancouver in the mid-1950s, changing accommodation. In a friend's house they meet an eccentric academic; then they experience an apparition of this person.

The third excerpt describes how the Woodcocks renovated their permanent home in the Kerrisdale district of Vancouver. In the process they experience a benign haunting and discover clues as to its former inhabitants.

The fourth excerpt is set, not in Canada, but on a working holiday on the French Riviera. In Menton, France, George experienced an inner anguish and perhaps an "angelic" visitation.

The fifth and final excerpt evokes the imagery of a significant dream which takes place in the Vancouver General Hospital in 1967 when he has a close encounter with death.

1.

WE SAID GOODBYE to our friends. Orwell was now in a sanatorium in Gloucestershire, and it is one of my enduring regrets that we did not have time at the end to go down and visit him. Herbert Read and Muriel Spark, Roy Fuller and Julian Symons, Mervyn Peake and Tambimuttu, all shook their heads and declared we would soon be back; Mulk Raj Anand made the jesting prophecy that we would meet next in India, which turned out to be true. A week before we left I met Marie Louise and we talked long and affectionately, largely about her strange Italian childhood and the years of her father's exile. She was sad we were going, but accepted it as she had eventually accepted my withdrawal from anarchist activism. We decided we would write letters to each other telling about our respective childhoods which some day we might publish as a dialogue. It was a way of continuing the collaboration we had both so valued.

So my wife and I took our train journey across the Midlands to Liverpool. The customs officers and the Special Branch men at the dockside searched our luggage to the last corner and the last page of every book. Then we went on our voyage over the stormy North Atlantic sea. As the great seas beat over the forward lounge I read Henry Mayhew's *London Labour and the London Poor*, which the American anthropologist Harold Orlans, a recently-acquired friend, had offered as a parting gift. We put into St. John's and went ashore, and then sailed on to Halifax, and lay in the harbour on the night of the 13th of April.

In a dream that night a male voice said to me, as I lay in an empty room, "Marie Louise is dead."

I dismissed it laughingly next morning. It took us five days to traverse Canada by train from Halifax to Vancouver and to cross on the ferry to Victoria. A cable awaited us there. Marie Louise was dead, from heart failure. The book I have finished, which is the first volume of my autobiography, is the substance of the letters I promised and at the time seemed to have no reason left to write.

2.

SINCE WE COULD no longer trespass on the Shadbolts' hospitality, we found a temporary home in Earle Birney's house on 3rd Avenue. Earle had already begun the series of absences that ended in his parting from Esther, and Esther offered us her basement, half of which was an immense games room we converted into a bed-sitting-room, and the other half a kitchen designed like a ship's galley by some former owner with a mania for boats. It even included an old ice-box, and we were among the last people in Vancouver to whom the iceman came twice a week with his great glassy block slung by immense tongs over his shoulder.

It was, at times, a turbulent house because of the presence in the attic of John Pearson, the original of the reprobate academic, John Parlabane in Robertson Davies' *The Rebel Angels*. John Pearson was almost as unbelievable as his fictional counterpart. He was a stocky man, running to fat, with a square, pugnacious, boyish but ravaged face whose resemblance to Churchill's he would accentuate by wearing a white yachting cap, which went with a gold-headed cane. He was a homosexual, an alcoholic, and a waywardly brilliant man, and all three features had combined to foster a bizarre existence; he had been a novice monk in an Anglican Benedictine monastery in England, but had gone over the wall after being disciplined for getting drunk on the sacramental wine. He had held a professorship of philosophy at a prairie university until he was expelled for his sins against propriety, and by the time we knew him he was an academic pariah whom no college would employ.

Yet he was extremely learned in strange fields. I had fine times with him, when he was relatively sober, discussing the history and doctrines of those Bulgarian heretics, the Bogomils. Since I was studying the Russian Doukhobors, we enjoyed dwelling on the similarities between the two sects and the possibilities of early contacts between them. In fact, John convinced me that Doukhoborism had its roots among the Bogomils, and I still give the idea a cautious credence.

Robertson Davies gives his character Parlabane a rather Mephistophelian quality, but any devilry John Pearson may have had was worn away by the time I knew him. He lived with all the furtive cunning of the inveterate alcoholic. Often, at night, we would be awakened while he rummaged like a great clumsy pack rat in the maze of pipes and airducts in the basement where he hid the bottles he sneaked into the house. Esther hit on manual work as a possible therapy, and allowed John to install in the garage a power saw with which he would cut the planks, out of which he began to construct neat, enormous pieces of furniture. The critical moments came when drinking and woodworking coincided. Some evenings we would stand on the lawn in the darkness, looking with tingling apprehension into the lit garage, where John in his yachting cap, reeling drunk, would be pushing planks into the saw. We did not dare go in, lest we scare him into a clumsy movement, and we decided that to cut off the power might be equally perilous, so we waited like Milton's servants, in case we might have to rush in and give first aid before the ambulance arrived. But the god that preserves drunkards always kept him from falling into that saw. When, after three months, we left for an apartment we had found in North Vancouver, Pearson was also departing, and we saw him only once again — or seemed to see him — under very odd circumstances.

This was almost three years later, towards the end of 1958. We were living in yet another apartment near the University. Our kitchen window overlooked a large corner lot occupied by a gas station, and one day, looking through the Venetian blinds, I saw John Pearson crossing the lot on the arm of a middle-aged woman.

Walk, carriage, face, yachting cap, gold-headed cane: there was no doubt of it. I called Inge and said: "Look! Johnny's back in Vancouver!" She came, also looked and also recognized him. Three weeks later we ran into Esther Birney at a party, and I remarked casually: "We saw Johnny Pearson the other day." She looked startled. Then she said: "You couldn't possibly have seen him. He shot himself in Toronto three months ago!"

3.

THAT SUMMER OF 1959 we worked hard giving our character to the house. The Cockney painter introduced us to a Cornish carpenter and handyman, taciturn and capable, and we worked with him, tearing down partitions to open out the upper floor, rebuilding the porches, refitting the bathroom, changing dog-chewed doors, laying sisal carpeting everywhere, and at the same time, by awakening it with good bone-white paint, reviving the touch of late Georgian elegance which the original carpenter-builder had given to the exterior.

The house had inhabitants as well as us. It was haunted. The manifestations were not visual, but aural and olfactory. We would hear a crack in the air, close to us, as if someone were snapping his fingers near our ears, and sometimes the clear light ringing of a silver bell, again elusively unplaceable but always high in the air. As soon as I started teaching, I developed the habit of writing far into the night, when I had finished preparing next day's classes and the telephone was silent, and Inge would often sit up doing her own work until we had decided it was time, at three or four in the morning, to go to bed. Then we were most often aware of the olfactory haunting, which took the form of both of us, often in separate rooms, suddenly noticing smells for which there was no immediate physical cause. The odours were in a restricted spectrum: cakes baking; bacon frying; fresh violets (in all seasons); and the ammoniacal sweetness of horse urine. The domestic associations of cakes and bacon were obvious; there were clumps of white violets in the garden, so that some former owner must have had a liking for that flower; the smell of horse urine puzzled me until,

reconstructing the basement, I found a crawlhole dense with cob-
webs under the back porch in which there were chains and bits of
harness; at some time, perhaps while the cottage still belonged to
the McCleery farm, someone who worked with cart horses had
lived here. The hauntings never went beyond sound and smell. No
spectre appeared, no voices spoke, and no identifying clue was
offered. All we knew was that the ghosts were benevolent, and we
felt happy when they manifested themselves, saying to each other,
as if we were spying on flesh-and-blood neighbours: "They're
baking cakes tonight," or, "The horse has just been pissing."

After a while the hauntings diminished. The sounds ceased first,
and then the smells came less frequently, though even now, late at
night, my nose will sometimes be tantalized with the smell of well-
cured bacon. We often wonder about this quiescence. Is it because
the presences are pleased with the way we have treated their house
and no longer need to draw anxious attention to themselves? Or is
it perhaps because, over the years, our introduction of more and
more religious images, masks, and paintings from India and Tibet
and from various animist cultures has created a spiritual barrier
which they are shy to penetrate?

4.

IN THE KIND of life in which I should have been happy, and Inge
was, I went through the darkest inner crisis of my life. The problem
was within myself, and it led me into deepest despair. I was lonely in
Menton, for we found it impossible to strike up personal relation-
ships with the local French. Our conversations did not go far
beyond the tradespeople, the postman, the concierge, and a couple
of the neighbours. And through the winter our only visitors were
Bert and Jessie Binning, who delighted us by arriving on Christmas
Eve.

I also found it hard to write at first, because of a lassitude that
was a reaction from the hard work of the preceding year. But after
Christmas the book on Peru went forward quickly, so that I was
able to finish it by the end of March, as well as reading many
French novels, writing articles for *Encounter* and *Tamarack*

Review on French fiction, and in *Arts* of New York on Mexican muralists. Yet even when the writing went well, I was still engulfed in a despair I could only keep at bay by working.

The crisis came in March. Inge's parents visited us, and she accompanied them for a brief trip to Italy while I stayed in Menton to finish my book. I became seized with a deep foreboding of death. No physical symptoms justified such a feeling, yet it was so strong that I did not think I would be alive when the others returned. I lay in panic, feeling that I would not even survive until the morning and that if death did not come in some other way I would have to kill myself. I was filled with fear, physically trembling with agitation, when I became aware of a presence inhabiting the room. It was not tangible or visible; it never spoke. I felt and knew its reality, yet what I knew and felt I could not describe except to say that it emanated peace. My agitation quietened until I was calm. The thought of death receded. I fell asleep and woke at dawn to walk along the seafront and enjoy everything I saw with the intensity of a reborn vision. I went home and confidently wrote the last pages of my book. Was I saved by some benign impulse emerging from my own unconscious and projecting itself into my surroundings? Was I visited by an angelic presence? I have always been content to accept it as inexplicable, just as it was invisible and intangible.

With spring the loneliness was broken.

5.

I HAD GIVEN six lectures on Homer which I am convinced were the best in my teaching career. During the last of them I had two slight spells of dizziness as I stood talking at the podium, but they passed and I thought no more about them until, at three in the morning, I felt a hard pain searing up my arm and into my jaw and gripping my chest in a relentless vice. I knew what was happening, and I felt detached as I told Inge and she went to call our doctor. I then lay wondering, for I had always thought myself a coward and had imagined that faced with a threat of death, I would be paralyzed with fear. Instead, I felt an equanimity, somewhat troubled by the thought of the difficulties for others my death might cause, and an immense curiosity. "Here it comes — and what afterwards?"

I was taken to the Vancouver General Hospital and that night, after I had been dosed with morphine and put in an oxygen tent, I had a dream that remains vividly with me. I was on a train rather like the old-fashioned trains surviving from the Empire that we had travelled on in Malaya and Ceylon; it was running beside a wide river I knew to be the Mekong. I got up from the bunk, dressed and began to pack an overnight bag, since I knew I was reaching my destination. There seemed to be no one else on the train; evidently it was running for me only. By the time I had dressed, the train began to slow and I saw it was approaching a wharf beside which a large white steamboat was moored. Even before the train stopped I was leaping down, but as my foot struck the platform the boat gave a single mournful hoot, swung away from the wharf and began to steam across the river to the town of white pagodas and pinnacles on the other side. I felt both relieved and bitterly disappointed as I got back into the train, which immediately sped into the fading of the dream.

The dream, of course, was telling me that it was not yet time for the release from life that is implied in the Buddhist symbolism of the Other Shore. Though there were still anxious days when I was kept in my oxygen tent under sedatives, enjoying the strange geometrical hallucinations induced by barbiturates, I at least knew that this time I was walking safely through the valley of the shadow, and I feared no evil.

Not entirely perversely I enjoyed my month in hospital, which still stays as a strange quiet island in my memory. I was forced out of the obsessive pattern of work I had developed. I read books unconnected with my work. I listened to music a great deal on a radio Inge had brought in. I valued the visits of my friends.

14. The Case of the Snoring Ghost

Margery Wighton

Margery Wighton, a Vancouver-based journalist, is the contributor of this account of a haunting. It was published under the title "The Case of the Haunted House and Snoring Ghost" in The Vancouver Sun on 27 Dec. 1952. No doubt the editors decided that a "snoring ghost" made delightful reading between Christmas and New Year's Day, Marley's ghost and all that!

For drawing my attention to the existence of this reminiscence, I am indebted to Eiran Harris who now lives in Montreal. During the 1960s, Harris lived in Vancouver where he worked as Canada's first ghostbuster. As an investigative reporter, in print and over the air, he drew attention to reports of hauntings in the Pacific Coast province, and he personally investigated a number of strange occurrences.

Harris did not have the opportunity to investigate Margery Wighton's account of "The Case of the Snoring Ghost." But he would smile at her suggestion that the haunted shack was erected over an old Indian burial ground. In the 1960s, whenever anyone reported "mystery lights," it was commonplace to suggest that the cause was "swamp gas." Nowadays, whenever a house in Canada is haunted, someone suggests that it was erected on an old Indian burial ground.

IT WAS THE EARLY SUMMER OF 1912. I was fifteen and living in British Columbia with my parents.

Quite unexpectedly, my father had a very good offer for our fruit farm in the Okanagan Valley, and we moved to Vancouver Island where he intended to start a poultry farm. We bought twelve acres of uncleared bush and arranged for the delivery of a sectional bungalow.

The problem was to find somewhere to live for about eight weeks while the bungalow was under construction. This matter was soon solved by the offer of a shack, belonging to a farmer, standing on the other side of a deep ravine, amid giant fir trees and thick undergrowth.

For the first few days, things were normal enough, and tired with helping my father unravel the plans of our bungalow, we came home each evening, and after supper were only too pleased to go to bed.

The third night, I went upstairs about nine o'clock and, while undressing, my mother sat on my bed talking to me. We had left my father reading in the little sitting-room. In the middle of her conversation, my mother stopped abruptly and laughed. My father was snoring downstairs!

"Daddy must be tired," she said. We both listened to a comfortable, monotonous snore, so distinct one would have imagined the sleeper to be in the room.

My mother rose and walked downstairs and I followed in my dressing-gown. "I thought you were asleep," she said. "We heard you snoring."

My father was indignant. "You must both be mad," he said. "I'm reading a good book."

We came upstairs again, and no sooner had I taken off my dressing-gown than we realized the snore was continuing. "Really," my mother said, "Daddy must be teasing us."

We laughed to relieve the tension, took off our shoes, and crept downstairs again, thinking to find my father pretending to snore. To our astonishment, we found him, as before, busy reading.

He looked annoyed and took off his glasses. "If you two think this is awfully amusing, I don't," he said.

The laughter died from our lips. We told him about the snoring.

He said we were still crazy and reluctantly followed us upstairs. And there it was again! Just a quiet, peaceful human snore.

"There's someone in here!" my father exclaimed, getting up impatiently. "But where?" he asked, looking around the bare walls, where there wasn't even a cupboard.

We banged about, thumping the walls, hitting the wooden ceiling. We moved the bed and table around but the snoring continued. We ransacked the second bedroom, but as we passed through the doorway we could not hear it any more.

My father went to the little kitchen at the foot of the stairs, while my mother and I stood at the top. We said "there" each time the snore came. He could not hear anything downstairs at all.

We then decided it must be something outside. But as we stood together outside the little shack, there was not a sound to be heard but the far-away cry of a night bird in the bush.

My father then stood under my low bedroom window, while my mother and I went back to my room. The snoring went on unabated but my father could hear nothing whatever.

Completely nonplussed, my mother and I went to bed in the second bedroom. My father determined not to sleep till he had "laid the ghost."

The moon shone through the windows and I found myself unable to sleep. At 2:00 a.m., my father came into the room. "I'm damned if I can stand it," he said. "I've tried everything to stop that snore. I thought I'd found one of you two snoring now."

Next day he and the owner raked the roof from end to end. That was really all they could do, since there was no loft and the place had no foundations. We could see under the flooring boards and there was absolutely nothing.

When evening came, the owner returned to see if he could hear the snoring, and sure enough it started again most punctually. Night after night our "snorer" enjoyed his slumbers while we had little rest.

People suggested owls, deer, chipmunks, spiders, and Indian tom-toms. But outside suggestions were disposed of, since once you left my bedroom you could hear nothing.

My father couldn't stand it and slept downstairs, while mother and I nervously occupied the second bedroom.

And we stood this for six weeks, with no hope of solving the mystery. Then our architect friend, Clem Webb, arrived. We told him all about our snoring ghost.

We congregated in the little bedroom once more, as we had done so often. Nine o'clock came, nine-thirty, ten. Nothing happened, for the first time in six weeks!

Clem Webb never heard it. He completely laid the ghost, and we never heard it again. We moved into our own bungalow about three weeks after his arrival, and almost forgot all about it.

But a year later, the owner of the shack wrote to a Vancouver firm for a new car. When it arrived, driven by a man from the garage, he decided he must have a few lessons before allowing the man to return to Vancouver. Having no room for him in the house, he put the driver to sleep in the haunted shack.

At midnight there was a wild knocking on his door and there stood the driver trembling from head to foot.

"The place is haunted," the man kept repeating. "I heard some-one come in, although I locked the door, walk upstairs and throw his boots off. Then the next thing I knew he was snoring loudly. Yet there's not a soul there, I went all round with a lamp."

He refused to return and left next morning.

The shack was still standing in its lonely setting among the tall dark pines when I visited the place in 1937. It was empty and had been for some years, people said.

I wandered once more through the deep gully, along the trail over the dried pine needles. The maple leaves had turned a bur-nished gold, and no one standing in that quiet spot would ever dream that such a disturbing mystery haunted the little shack.

Perhaps the Indians are nearest the truth. They say it's built over an old Indian burial ground.

Who knows?

15. A Warning

Hazel L. Mack

"A *Warning" is the title Hazel L. Mack chose for this personal account of the appearance of a forerunner. It is written in a straightforward manner about an incident that took place some forty years ago. How vivid it remains in the correspondent's memory!*

Mrs. Mack is a researcher and writer, based in Guelph, Ont., who has contributed accounts of some of her other unusual experiences to Fate Magazine. *As well, she contributed a memoir about the sighting of a most unusual UFO to* Extraordinary Experiences *(1989), the first volume in this series of books devoted to paranormal Canadiana.*

The present account was accompanied by a letter dated 15 March 1990 and addressed to the present editor. In her letter Mrs. Mack wrote as follows:

> *I remember being very "keyed" up that day and I was driving much faster than I usually did. My late husband paid little attention to any ideas I had. He had no belief either in psychic matters. I don't believe now that Mrs. Ware would have paid any attention to me either. She was originally from London, England, and had far different ideas from those that I have. In Canada, she became a farmer's wife. She may secretly not have liked her position. It was "something" to see this all-black*

*figure walking down the farm laneway. I wish I under-
stood better such things.*

*Mrs. Mack expresses a desire that no doubt every reader of her
account wishes were possible.*

IT HAPPENED IN THE LATE AUTUMN of 1952, a Saturday. My husband and I had been doing the various errands in preparation for the coming weekend.

We lived then in a forty-acre section of rich swampland that bordered the narrow Eramosa River. It was also a good farming area, one of the best in Wellington County. Our particularly well-treed area was always cool in summer and warm in winter. My husband cared for a large number of peafowl and ornamental pheasants. He did not drive a car, so I did many of the errands, often driving him where he wished to go.

On this particular day we had finished the shopping and were making good time, headed homeward, taking a short cut off No. 7 Highway on the 4th Line. Often a rough surface to drive on, there seemed to be more ruts than usual. The road went down to the edge of the Eramosa River, across a narrow bridge, and then we were climbing again.

I was driving fast despite the rough roads, for I knew my husband had an appointment awaiting him. We began to climb out of the valley. We were approaching the Ware farm on the left-hand side of the road. Looking up as we approached the driveway, I saw Mrs. Barbara Ware walking down towards the roadway, probably to their mailbox. To my amazement she appeared entirely black. I at once began to slow the car, for I intended to turn around when I saw a suitable place to turn and tell her how she had appeared to me. I had never spoken to Mrs. Ware for in a way I was a newcomer to the area some four years previously. Not being involved with farming in any way, we had never met.

"Keep going," my husband said impatiently. "We're already late."

Regretfully, I stepped up the speed of the car for I knew someone was waiting for him at home.

The afternoon work in my home kept me busy for some time,

but I kept thinking of Mrs. Ware. I had never met her. I had almost become acquainted with her sister a while previously when in Acton, but both girls were from England and did not seem to want to get acquainted.

I wanted to tell Mrs. Ware how she had appeared to me, although I had never seen anything like it previously. It seemed to me to be a warning, but finally I gave up on it, not being sure what all the blackness portended. I had become tired and it was too far to walk to her home. We had no telephone then so I couldn't warn her that way. Finally it all slipped out of my mind.

The next morning a relative arrived with the dreadful news. Mrs. Ware had been killed the evening before, seven hours after I had seen her.

There was nothing I could say to my husband. I felt he should not have minded that day if we were but a few minutes late. The distance was, of course, several miles by road.

Several years later I attended a meeting at the home of Dr. A. R. G. Owen, a well-known writer on matters pertaining to heredity, biometrics, nature, and parapsychology. His fairly recent book, Psychic Mysteries of Canada, is a fund of psychic knowledge. "What a shame you didn't go back and warn Mrs. Ware," Dr. Owen remarked.

Indeed it was, and I have never ceased to regret it.

16. The Gift of Sight

Patricia Pelky

Patricia Pelky wrote to me on 9 Aug. 1990 from Thunder Bay, Ont. In a carefully composed letter, she recalled some experiences which have remained in her memory and continue to perplex her.

The experiences are not all that extraordinary. Possible premonitions, unusually vivid dreams, etc. Mrs. Pelky's experiences could be attributable to coincidence. Or could they? Are other explanations possible? The reader may decide.

SOME TIME AGO I noticed your letter in *Lakehead Living* and began to wonder if I should write of my experiences. I've always felt a bit uncomfortable and hence have rarely mentioned them to anyone. However, I do think I have had several occurrences which are difficult to explain in terms of normal experiences.

These incidents, some of which could be attributed to coincidence, I will not mention. But two or three occasions in particular stand out as inexplicable in the ordinary course of events.

My father, with whom I was very close, died in October of 1958. Several months later I had an extremely vivid dream in which I was sitting with others in a room of one of our stately old houses. My father came in the door and there was a strong glow around his head and face. He did not speak but came over to me.

His hand was very warm and even when I woke in the morning I could still feel the heat in my own hands. I did not understand the meaning, if any, of this strange dream. A few months later, August 1959, my husband died at age thirty-seven. I cannot say if this was a case of precognition, but it almost seemed that my father was warning me and couldn't bear to look me in the eye. To this day I can remember every detail of that dream, though there have been many I couldn't describe later.

Pursuant to the incident, in June of 1959, my husband and two sons left one evening and returned in a large, blue station-wagon. He wished me to come for a ride, but for some reason I kept saying "no" though I did not know why. Something would not let me go, though ordinarily I would have gone without hesitation. Disappointed, he returned the car and we kept our old Plymouth. Only later, after his death in August, did it occur to me that I may have had some forewarning about his death that I didn't realize at the time. I always felt bad that I had let him down.

Some years previous to the above incidents, there was another occasion in which I seemed to have been aware of something wrong without actually knowing what had happened. Early in the war, the Algonquin Regiment was stationed here, and I met some of the lads at our church's Young People's Club.

One young man in particular I fell in love with and for several months we went out together. As it turned out, I learned he was married and the romance was over. I had, however, felt very strongly for him at the time and took a while to get over it. Later, after I had been happily married for several years, with two small sons, I began to think of Dan for about a week. I could not seem to put thoughts of him aside, no matter how hard I tried. They kept creeping into my mind though I kept telling myself "forget him."

At the end of the week, my sister telephoned me and asked if I had seen the newspaper of the previous weekend and, in particular, the column regarding accidents in the province. Although I usually read it, I had somehow missed it. It turned out that Dan, who was a bush pilot in Haileybury, flying fishing parties, geologists, etc., had been returning from a flight and encountered a squall on the lake just as he landed his float plane. Although he was a strong swimmer, he must have been trapped somehow and went down with his plane.

I trust these incidents are of some interest and may assist in your research. By the way, I have Celtic blood on both sides of my family. Do you suppose I have "the gift of sight"?

17. I Saw the Outline of the Head

Carol Goodger-Hill

Carol Goodger-Hill, a resident of Waterloo, Ontario, sent me the following account of an extremely vivid childhood memory. She sent it to me on 24 June 1990 after reading my request for "ghost stories" which appeared in The Guelph Daily Mercury.

Ms. Goodger-Hill added, "I tried to set it down a few years ago and you may find the telling somewhat dramatic for your purposes. At any rate, here it is. I should add that we left the house when I was fifteen and it is now, I understand, a sort of half-way house for people who are trying to recover from drugs. I rather wonder what they make of the place."

WHEN I WAS A CHILD we always went away on Labour Day weekend. The trip was in some ways an ordeal. My parents were always nervous to be far from home and longed to be back. I could not bear to be cooped up for hours in a car with nothing to do, and after dark, nothing to see. It would be late when we finally drove into the back yard. We would gather up our things and without saying much, go into the house, happy to be away from each other.

The year before, when I was nine, I had bounded up the darkened staircase towards my room at the back of the second floor. I had to go through an upstairs hall and my parents' room to reach my small back bedroom. I discovered that while I had been away part of the ceiling above my bed had fallen. It lay in heavy chunks on the pillow and the blanket. I had been frightened, but my mother had reminded me that the house was very old. The ceiling had been cracked. She felt it was a lucky chance that had kept me from home when it fell.

Now, a year later, I again ran up the hairpin staircase. The moonlight lay cold and white across the upstairs hall. I hesitated a moment in the hall, but went on into my parents' room. I was part way across the room before I became aware that I was not alone. By the window, in the moonlight, someone sat in the chair and watched me. I saw the outline of the head and a glow; I saw the eyes and I felt a dread that gripped the back of my neck and froze my hair.

Without a thought, I turned in mid-step and tore back the way I had come, clattering and calling down the staircase. I met my mother in the downstairs hall and tried to make her understand that something was in her bedroom. Compressing her lips, my mother made me retrace my steps and go back upstairs with her. Swiftly she crossed the hall and flipped on the light. In the sudden glare, the room was neat and empty. The window was black. The chair had nothing worse on it than a castoff housecoat.

Together we went over to my room and turned on the light. After its collapse a year earlier, the ceiling had been repaired and my bed had been moved. In horror, I saw that once more the ceiling was down. Once again my bed was littered with large, heavy chunks of plaster. Above it the lathes were bare. There was no other damage in the house.

After many years I still have no explanation for that night. My mother, unrelenting, matter-of-fact, believed it was all a coincidence. She still believes that. All the time we lived in that house, she found it comfortable. She could walk through it from cellar to attic without a light, if she thought she heard a strange noise in the night. She never had a bad experience. The rest of the family were not so brave.

The back bedroom remained mine for two more years. Usually it was peaceful, but some nights I lay awake in terror of something that I could not name. After two years, I inherited the west bedroom. For some reason the atmosphere on that side of the house was more benign. In the years that followed, that bedroom was my island of peace. Often, when the rest of the family was out, I would sit behind the closed door, listening to the house live around me. I knew that so long as I stayed there quietly, I would be safe.

18. The Root Cellar

Janet Lunn

*J*anet Lunn *is a writer of fine books for young readers. Among her bestselling titles are* Double Spell *(1968) and* The Root Cellar *(1980). The first of these novels, appropriately, has two titles, for it is about "doubles." Some readers may know it under its American title* Twin Spell.

The second of her novels is relevant here. A short while ago a librarian told me that Lunn based The Root Cellar *on an actual incident that occurred in her house in Hillier, a small community which lies southeast of Trenton in the Bay of Quinte region. Hillier is located close to Consecon, the community that gave birth to the famous or infamous Fox Sisters, the foremost spiritualists of the second half of the 19th century.*

Now, ghosts in fictional works are products of the literary imagination, not products of powers in the spirit-world. So I wrote to Lunn to ask her if it is true that when she wrote The Root Cellar *she was basing her work of fiction on a real-life event. She wrote back right away. I have reproduced her letter of reply in full.*

Lunn ends her letter with two questions. The last question is easily answered. Yes, the description is helpful — and I hope it will introduce more readers to Lunn's novels. The first question is less easily answered. She refers to Canadian Literary Landmarks, *my guidebook to sites in Canada with literary associations. It is true that the book has only a handful of references to children's books. Why this is so, I am no longer sure. Certainly there will be more should the book go into a second edition.*

December 28, 1988

DEAR JOHN,

The house with the ghost is the house I live in. It is an old house, the oldest part is about 170 years, the rest newer, built in stages ending around 1890-1900. I am not the one who has seen or heard the ghost (it could be ghosts, of course). Richard, my late husband, saw her on one occasion, the silhouette of a woman in a long dress and a bonnet. She came into the room that was, in former times, a parlour, leaned over as if to put something on a table then disappeared.

Dick sometimes felt a presence in the house and on one occasion heard a woman humming in the kitchen. When he went to investigate, the humming had stopped and there was no one there. We have all heard footsteps on the stairs and another room in the house unnerves all the dogs who go there.

I have no doubt that there is at least one ghost here in spite of the fact that I have not seen any myself. I do think some people are sensitive to ghosts and some aren't.

Yes, I did use Dick's ghost-seeing incident in a book. It was in *The Root Cellar* which is set in this house. In fact, the whole story turns on the incident and the ghost is one of the major characters. As for it — or any other of my books — being famous, I feel flattered, of course, but I can't help but scold you a little. If Canadian children's books are to be considered famous, why are Canadian children's writers not included in your book about Canadian literary geography?

Will this description help you?

Cheers,
Janet Lunn

19. The Man Had Just Disappeared

Michaeleen Berger

Michaeleen Berger, a resident of Paris, Ontario, saw my letter requesting "ghost stories" in the Brant News, *and sent me the following response. I am reproducing it as she wrote it.*

It is interesting to note the fact that experiences of this sort seem to occur at dawn and at dusk, often in surroundings new to the observer, when the conscious mind is either waking from deep sleep or falling into deep sleep. Psychologists refer to such perceptions or misperceptions as hypnagogic and hypnopompic experiences. Parapsychologists suggest that such experiences occur to human beings when they are in altered states of consciousness and hence accessible to other realities.

June 6, 1990

DEAR JOHN:

I've always wanted to write a Dear John letter...(sorry, couldn't help it!).

I read your letter in the *Brant News* and thought you might be interested in my experience. It happened to me once. It never happened to me before or after.

My husband and I bought an old house, and the night we moved in I had this experience. My husband worked the night shift from 11:00 p.m. to 7:00 a.m. I worked around the house till about two o'clock, emptying boxes, etc.

When I went to bed, I fell asleep right away. I half awoke when I felt my husband getting into bed early that morning. I was still very tired so I rolled over in bed to face him and put my hand up to his face to give him a pat on the cheek.

My hand encountered his nose. My fingers went along the bridge of his nose, and I remember thinking, "That's not Rod's nose...." Rod has worn glasses all his life, and when he takes them off they leave a mark on the bridge of his nose.

My fingers went up and down this nose, and it felt too long and it had a sharp ridge to it. I sat up in bed, really frightened, and turned to see who was in bed beside me.

The man was about fifty years old with a receding hairline. His hair was salt and pepper and cut real short. He was lying there and smiling at me.

I jumped out of bed and said, "Who are you?" He just lay there and smiled. (We didn't have our phone in yet, or I'd have called the police.) I ran to the bathroom and locked the door. I thought, "Well, I can't stay in here the rest of the night. I've got to get rid of him somehow."

So, armed with a can of Lysol, I went back into the bedroom, but he wasn't there. I looked under the bed, for that was the only place he could hide. (We didn't even have any closets built yet.)

The man had just disappeared! Then I thought, "Maybe I'm dreaming this." I pinched myself hard — and it hurt like blazes. But the shock didn't seem to wake me up, so to speak, so I just couldn't be sleepwalking!

An hour later, after I'd had a cup of tea and calmed myself down, I said to myself that I was probably overtired and that I had dreamed the whole thing.

I went back to the bedroom and got into bed. As I was pulling the covers up, I looked over at the other pillow. There was a dent in it, as if a person's head had lain there....

Michaeleen Berger

20. This Was Definitely Out of Character

Sharon Steele

Sharon Steele is a resident of Chatham, Ont., who has a musical bent. She saw my request for "extraordinary experiences" in the pages of The London Free Press. She wrote to me and assessed that my interest in the paranormal was serious, so she sent me this account of half a lifetime punctuated with odd and inexplicable experiences.

Mrs. Steele's account is dated 6 June 1990, and it is reproduced here in the form in which it was written with only routine copy editing. After reading the account, one is left with questions. Is Mrs. Steele a genuinely psychic person? Does she attract to herself, does she "collect," such experiences? Is there someone or something in her past that refuses to go away? Is there a middle-aged woman, a witch, a spectre, someone or something that plays the piano and sings "Ave Maria"? Has she seen the last of this spirit?

EVEN AS A CHILD, I was aware of unexplainable phenomena, as I had two grandmothers who not only seemed to have a "sixth sense," but who actually "spoke" to people who weren't there. Some would say such activity was attributable to senility or to being "not wrapped too tight." But, around our house, it didn't seem strange at all!

I remember stories my parents used to relate about their respective mothers' abilities. My maternal grandmother was known for her unconventional conversations with people from the Other Realm, while my paternal grandmother had the extraordinary power of "seeing" things as they happened. In one instance, my father related how, at the age of about twenty, he was involved in a motorcycle accident and hurt his nose. It was subsequently bandaged at the hospital. Upon arriving home, being quite late, he quietly entered the house through the door into the room in which his parents slept. (I should clarify that this happened in Jamaica quite some time ago, and with eight children, each room in the house was used to its fullest extent.)

As he was passing by the bed, his mother called out, "What has happened to your nose?" This wouldn't ordinarily seem odd except that her back was to him at the time and it was so dark that he had been feeling his way around. When he explained he was fine, just a minor accident, she replied, "I know. I saw it."

On another occasion, when my father was younger, he had an even younger brother who came down with a case of spinal meningitis which, at that time, was difficult to diagnose and impossible to treat. When he became ill in the morning, he was taken to the local hospital, quite some distance away. Later in the day, his mother, who had been ironing in the kitchen, suddenly and quietly put the iron down and announced, "Roland has just passed." The family knew better than to question the statement. It was about four o'clock. Sometime after six that evening, the knock on the door came. (There was no telephone.) A policeman on his bicycle had arrived with a message from the hospital. Their son Roland had passed away at four o'clock that afternoon. No one was surprised.

After hearing these stories about our family, it really didn't seem strange when I saw my first ghost. I was about thirteen. I had come home from school for lunch and was in the living-room waiting for my girlfriend to pick me up when, out of the corner of my eye, I saw movement. I swung my head around and saw someone dressed in a mauve robe heading for the basement stairs. The person's back was to me, but I assumed it was my cousin who lived with us. I assumed she was home from work because she had been ill. I called her name and getting no answer, I figured she hadn't heard me, so I got up and walked to the doorway of the stairwell and called again.

Still no response, so I headed down the stairs. I reached the basement and called again. Silence. I searched that basement for five minutes and found no one. Whoever it had been had simply disappeared.

When I mentioned that incident in later years, I discovered I was not alone in my sighting. Apparently just about everyone who lived in the house had seen or heard this person!

Home, until I was fifteen, was Rexdale, Ont., but, just after I turned sixteen, we pulled up stakes and moved to Oakville. Things got interesting about a year after we moved in. At this point I should tell you that, until the age of thirteen, I had studied piano with the Royal Conservatory of Music in Toronto and played frequently, mostly classical pieces by Chopin, Beethoven, and company.

One morning, at breakfast, I was accosted by one of my sisters. "What were you doing playing the piano at three in the morning? Don't you know people are trying to sleep at that hour?" I guess I must have looked blank because she said, "Wasn't it you?" I shook my head and we continued to look at each other, wondering if anyone else had heard anything. The weird part of it was that my bedroom door was right across from the piano and I hadn't heard anything. And I thought I was a light sleeper! It wasn't long before just about everyone in the house had heard the music. My father tried to explain it away as crossed radio wires or an avid radio listener, but we knew better.

My younger sister's girlfriend received quite a surprise one afternoon. She used to come to our house at lunchtime every school day and wait for my sister to come so they could eat together. One day my sister arrived to find her friend practically cringing in the chair by the fireplace in the family room. She was as white as a sheet. My sister breezed into the room and — not known for her tact — exclaimed, "Hi! My God, you look like you've just seen a ghost!" Well, it seems her girlfriend had been treated to a concert of Mendelssohn. She had thought I was home from college and yelled out to me. When I didn't answer and the playing continued, she assumed I didn't hear her so she went to the basement door. The instant she opened the door the playing stopped. There wasn't a soul in sight. I was getting a little weary of taking the blame for this character. But in a way I was pleased. This person could really play!

In a more recent vein, about ten years ago my husband and I moved from Toronto to Chatham. We rented a house in a newer neighbourhood and subsequently bought the house four years later. During that time we were subjected to a few incidents, some of which weren't so pleasant. I started finding things in the oddest places. My purse was in the refrigerator one day. A few weeks later I found my watch in the cupboard under the sink. I thought I was losing it. Then about a month later my husband dropped me off at the dentist and returned home. When he came in the door, he said he heard a ticking sound like a clock, but the only clock that close by was a cuckoo clock that we had hung in the hallway for decoration only. The stupid thing had quit on us the day we put it up after the move from Toronto. It had worked beautifully until then.

Well, guess what decided to work after a couple of years of doing nothing? Not only that, but upon closer inspection, he found it was set to the correct time! When I arrived home, I couldn't believe what I was hearing. It even cuckooed! For four days it ran. Then it quit again and it was on to bigger things!

One evening I had gone to bed earlier than usual, and my husband had stayed downstairs to watch the eleven o'clock news as is our usual habit. He came upstairs around eleven-thirty or thereafter, and came into the room and touched my shoulder. I woke up startled. He was calling me and I answered, "What's the matter?" He asked me if I had been singing. (I sang with a couple of choirs and did some solo work at the time.) I asked him what on earth he was talking about. It would seem our ghost liked to sing — "Ave Maria."

Shortly thereafter, she either turned nasty or someone else came into the picture. I had two sons at the time, aged three and two years respectively. They slept in the same room. For almost three weeks, every night at about ten o'clock they would wake up in unison and begin to scream. This was definitely out of character for them, and I asked the older one out of earshot of the younger one why he was screaming. The older one replied that there was "a witch" in his room and that she was on fire. When the younger one was asked, he said (in his own language), "Bad mon'ter. Burn me, Mummy," and started to cry. This went on, as I said, for about three weeks and then stopped.

Finally, not long after that, it was afternoon and the kids and I were eating lunch in the kitchen when the two-year-old pointed to the kitchen door and said, "Who dat, Mummy?" I looked around just in time to see a figure fading away, almost like a mist dissipating. It was a woman; she was middle-aged, short, with wavy hair, dressed in a housedress that was worn back in the days of "Father Knows Best." She seemed to have been smiling.

From that day, we haven't had any problems. But every time something the least bit weird happens, we look at each other and say jokingly, "She's ba-a-ck...!"

21. The Haunting of Mackenzie House

Mackenzie House is one of the most historic buildings in Toronto. Since 1960 it has been maintained as a museum by the Toronto Historical Board. Despite the fact that Mackenzie House has been called the most haunted house in Toronto — and perhaps the most haunted house in all of Canada — it is the policy of the Board to maintain that Mackenzie House is not haunted. Guides dressed in period costume who escort visitors through its halls and rooms, which are furnished to recall the period of the 1860s, make no mention of reports of ghosts or poltergeists or mysterious happenings.

Today the residence bears the proud name of William Lyon Mackenzie (1795-1861). Mackenzie is remembered as the energetic publisher of the Colonial Advocate, the first Mayor of the City of Toronto in 1834, the promoter of responsible government, and the leader of the Rebellion of 1837 in Upper Canada. He is affectionately recalled as "the little rebel" and "the firebrand."

When the rebellions in Upper and Lower Canada were suppressed, Mackenzie in the garb of a woman fled the city, finding refuge first on Navy Island in the Niagara River and then in the State of New York where he continued his agitation. With the general amnesty for participants in the Rebellions, he and his wife Isabel and their large family returned to Toronto in triumph.

The three-storey brick residence at 82 Bond Street, which dates from the early 1850s, was acquired by public subscription and presented to Mackenzie in recognition of his public service. He lived *in the house from 1857 to his sad decline and death of "apoplectic seizure" on 28 Aug. 1861. Isabel Baxter Mackenzie, his loyal wife, died in the house on 12 Jan. 1873. Isabel Grace King, their thirteenth and last child, was born in exile in the United States but spent her childhood years in the house. She went on to marry the lawyer John King and they made their home at Woodside, outside Berlin (now Kitchener), Ont. She died at Kingsmere in the Gatineau region of Quebec, in 1917. The Kings raised a family of two girls and two boys; the most prominent of their children was William Lyon Mackenzie King.*

William Lyon Mackenzie King (1874-1950), the grandson of William Lyon Mackenzie, was born at Woodside. The grandson took great pride in his grandfather's commitment to responsible government. He studied law and went on to become (in 1921) the tenth Prime Minister of Canada and the country's most curious citizen and the British Commonwealth and Empire's longest-lasting leader.

It is now known that throughout his life spiritualism held a great fascination for Mackenzie King. The question of human survival after death perplexed him. Indeed, one of his friends, the correspondent Percy J. Philip, claimed in 1954 that the ghost of Mackenzie King had joined him and had conversed with him for some time on a park bench at Kingsmere, Mackenzie King's country estate in the Gatineau region of Quebec. His spiritualistic beliefs and practices are ably documented, notably by the historian C. P. Stacey in A Very Double Life: The Private World of Mackenzie King *(1976). But the views of his grandfather, William Lyon Mackenzie, have gone unrecorded; yet it is difficult to believe that the grandfather, being of Scottish birth and ancestry, was unfamiliar with the subject of the supernatural.*

There are no reports of any psychical occurrences in Mackenzie House prior to 1956; there are none of substance subsequent to 1966. These years cover a period of time that corresponds to two events: the centenary of the occupancy of the house by the two Mackenzies; the public campaign to acquire the house, led by the Mackenzie Homestead Foundation, and the assumption of ownership and operation of the House by the Toronto Historical Board. The accounts of mysterious disturbances within the house come from the two caretaking couples who occupied the building during this period of transition.

The first caretakers were Mr. and Mrs. Charles Edmunds. They occupied Mackenzie House from 13 Aug. 1956 to April 1960, and left only because of the disturbances. They were followed by Mr. and Mrs. Alex Dobban who arrived in April and left in June 1960, complaining of the same disturbances. Andrew MacFarlane, enterprising feature writer for the Toronto Telegram, broke the story of the hauntings and published the principal accounts, most notably the affidavits of the Edmunds family.

The rival newspaper, the Toronto Star, requested that Archdeacon John Frank of Holy Trinity Anglican Church conduct the rite of exorcism. He did so in the presence of reporters on 2 July 1960. Thereafter the house's caretakers have lived off the premises, but from time to time maintenance workers and visitors to the house have registered complaints of disturbances. The suggestion has always been in the air that the disturbances were so much "hot air," that the Mackenzie Homestead Foundation encouraged the reports of mysterious distrubances to draw public attention to Mackenzie House and its own campaign to preserve it for posterity.

The most intelligent discussion — and debunking — of the ghostly happenings at Mackenzie House was conducted by Joe Nickell in one chapter of his book Secrets of the Supernatural: Investigating the World's Occult Mysteries (Buffalo: Prometheus Books, 1988). Nickell is both a professional stage magician and a licensed private investigator. He has both prosaic and highly imaginative explanations for all the disturbances. Although he writes well, the story he has to tell is not as gripping as the stories that have been told by members of the Edmunds family.

Mr. and Mrs. Charles Edmunds, the first caretaking couple, lived in the house for four years. Their reports are included here, as are the shorter reports of their son Robert and his wife Minnie who were frequent guests in the house. These reports first appeared in Andrew MacFarlane's series of articles in the Toronto Telegram under the general title "The Ghosts that Live in Toronto" published on June 27, 28, and 29, 1960. The series appeared following the refusal of the Dobbans to remain in the *house. MacFarlane secured sworn affidavits from the Edmunds. All the statements are reproduced here in minimally edited form.*

Added to MacFarlane's accounts is yet another first-hand account. This one is by Roger Chicoine, a non-resident custodian of the house in 1962 and 1963. On occasion, Chicoine slept overnight in the house. He described his experiences to the journalist Clarke Wallace who recorded them in his article "Historic House with Distinguished Ghost" which appeared in Weekend Magazine, *4 May 1963. Chicoine said that on four occasions he saw visions of a grave lady in white, the spirit of Isabel Baxter Mackenzie. It is interesting to note that both MacFarlane and Wallace also spent nights in Mackenzie House, but on these occasions the spirits were shy and failed to appear or be heard.*

1. Mrs. Charles Edmunds

FROM THE FIRST DAY my husband and I went to stay at the Mackenzie Homestead, we could hear footsteps on the stairs when there was nobody in the house but us.

The first day, when I was alone in the house, I could hear someone clearly, walking up the stairs from the second floor to the top. Nearly every day there were footsteps at times when there was no one there to make them.

One night I woke up at midnight. I couldn't sleep, although I am normally a good sleeper. I saw a Lady standing over my bed. She wasn't at the side, but at the head of the bed, leaning over me. There is no room for anyone to stand where she was. The bed is pushed up against the wall.

She was hanging down, like a shadow, but I could see her clearly. Something seemed to touch me on the shoulder to wake me up. She had long hair hanging down in front of her shoulders, not black or gray or white, but dark brown, I think. She had a long narrow face. Then it was gone.

Two years ago, early in March, I saw the Lady again. It was the same — except this time she reached out and hit me. When I woke up, my left eye was purple and bloodshot.

I also saw the man at night, a little bald man in a frock coat. I would just see him for a few seconds, and then he would vanish.

I often saw one or the other standing in the room — at least eight or nine times.

A year ago last April, I told my husband: "I have to get out of here." I had to get out of that house. If I didn't get out, I knew I'd be carried out in a box.

I think it was the strain all the time that made me feel this way. I went from 130 pounds to 90½ pounds. I wasn't frightened, but it was getting my nerves down.

It was just like knowing there was someone watching you from behind all the time, from just over your shoulder.

Sometimes we'd sit watching the television. My husband might look up all of a sudden at the doorway. I knew what it was. You felt that someone had just come in.

My son and his wife heard the piano playing at night when they were staying with us. When my husband and my son went to look — it stopped.

We could feel the homestead shaking with a rumbling noise some nights. It must have been the press in the basement. We thought at first it might be the subway. But we were too far from the subway....

I did not believe in ghosts when I went to stay at the Mackenzie Homestead. But I do now. It's the only explanation I can think of.

I wish to say that I would not say anything against the Mackenzies. They were hard-working people and so are we. They were not hard on us...it's just that the house was a strain on the nerves.

2. Mr. Charles Edmunds

Certain happenings during the three years and eight months my wife and I served as caretakers of the Mackenzie Homestead have convinced me that there is something peculiar about the place.

On one occasion my wife and I were sleeping in the upstairs bedroom. She woke me up in the middle of the night and said that she had seen a man standing beside her bed.

My wife, to my certain knowledge, knew nothing of Mackenzie or his history. All of the pictures in the homestead show Mackenzie as a man with hair on his head. The man my wife saw and described to me was completely bald with side whiskers. I had read about Mackenzie. And I know that the man she described to me was Mackenzie. He wore a wig to cover his baldness. But she did not know this.

On another occasion, just after we moved in, my two grandchildren, Susan (then aged 4) and Ronnie (then aged 3) went from the upstairs bedroom down to the second-floor bathroom at night.

A few minutes later there were terrific screams. I went down and they were both huddled in the bathroom, terrified. They said there was a Lady in the bathroom. I asked where she was now and they said she just disappeared.

On another night my wife woke up screaming. She said: "There was a small man standing over my bed." She described Mackenzie.

Another night, a woman came up to the bed and looked at my missus. She was a little woman, about my wife's height. My wife said: "Dad — there was a woman here." I told her she was dreaming.

Another night my wife woke up and woke me. She was upset. She said the Lady had hit her. There were three red welts on the left side of her face. They were like finger marks. The next day her eye was bloodshot. Then it turned black and blue. Something hit her. It wasn't me. And I don't think she could have done it herself. And there wasn't anyone else in the house.

On another occasion something peculiar happened with some flowers we had in pots on a window ledge inside the house. This was in winter and we had the geraniums inside. We watered the plants twice a week on Sundays and Wednesdays.

On a Saturday morning we found that they had all been watered, although we hadn't done it. There was water spilled all over the plants and the saucers they were standing in were full. There was mud on the curtains, and holes in the earth as if someone had poked their fingers in the earth. There was water on the dressing-table. Neither of us had watered the plants, and neither had anyone else.

We often heard footsteps on the stairs. Thumping footsteps like someone with heavy boots on. This happened frequently when there was no one in the house but us, when we were sitting together usptairs.

The whole house used to shake with a rumbling sound some-times. My wife is convinced that this was Mackenzie's press.

I am not an imaginative man, and I do not believe in ghosts. But the fact is that the house was strange enough so that we had to leave.

We would have stayed if it had not been for these happenings. But my wife could not stand it any longer.

3. Mr. Robert Edmunds

One night my wife woke me up. She said she heard the piano playing downstairs. I heard it, too. I cannot remember what the music was like, but it was the piano downstairs playing.

Dad and I went downstairs. When we got to the last landing before the bottom the piano stopped.

It was similar with the printing press in the basement. My wife heard it first and wakened me. I heard it, too. I identified the sound because it was the same as old presses I'd seen in movies and on television. A rumbling, clanking noise — not like modern presses. When Dad and I went downstairs to see about it, it stopped when we reached the same landing.

We heard the piano three or four times, the press just once.

I was not walking in my sleep. I heard them. I don't know what the explanation is. I am not prepared to say I saw any ghosts or apparitions. But I can say that I dreamt more in that house than I ever have before or since.

I do not believe in ghosts. But I find it hard to explain what we heard.

4. Mrs. Minnie Edmunds

When my husband and I were staying at Mackenzie Homestead I heard the piano playing downstairs at night three or four times.

We discovered that there was no one downstairs to play it these times, and yet I heard it distinctly. Each time, I woke my husband, and when he and his father went downstairs to investigate it, it stopped.

On one other occasion I heard the printing press running in the basement. I woke my husband, and he and his father went to investigate it. It stopped.

It is not possible to operate the press, because it is locked, and on the occasions when I heard the piano, there was no one downstairs to play it. I can find no natural explanation for these occurrences.

5. Mr. Alex Dobbin

We couldn't stay any longer because of the effect the place was having on my wife's nerves. The things she heard were getting her down. We wouldn't have left otherwise; but she couldn't stand to stay overnight....

6. Mrs. Alex Dobbin

We hadn't been here long when I heard footsteps going up the stairs. I called to my husband. But he wasn't there. There was no one else in the house. But I heard feet on the stairs.

One night I woke up. There was a rumbling noise in the basement. At first I took it to be the oil burner. But my husband checked — and the furance wasn't on.

The noise I heard was the press. It's locked. But I heard it running. I heard it that night, and one or two other nights.

On another night I heard the piano in the front room downstairs playing, after we were in bed. There was no one else in the house, but the piano was playing. It wasn't a tune — just as if someone was hitting the keys with closed fists, or a child playing at the piano.... You see, it's locked. And yet I heard it running. How could you explain that.

There was no one else in the house, just the two of us.... It was coming from the basement. It was that press.... There's something in this house, and I'm not staying with it....

Yes, I do think it was a ghost. I didn't believe in that sort of thing before. But how else can you explain it?

7. Mr. Roger Chicoine

Don't get the idea I see Mrs. Mackenzie every time I sleep here. There's a good chance she doesn't like strangers....

The first time I saw Mrs. Mackenzie was right in that doorway. I awoke just at dawn and looked out the window. I remember thinking how stupid that was because I never wake at this time; about 5:00 or 6:00 a.m. Suddenly it seemed as though I wasn't alone in the room.

A chill went racing up and down my spine. I was lying with my hands under my head and I turned slowly, taking in the whole room. My eyes came to the door and there was a woman. I recognized her from the portrait: it was Mrs. Mackenzie.

She seemed to be leaning around the corner of the door for I could only see the top half of her. I felt the hair on my head start to stand straight up on its end. I blinked, but she didn't move.

She was not transparent. That is, I could not see the wall through her. She looked fleshy. Alive. Believe me, I thought it was all in my imagination, but she looked so real, this ghost. Finally I moved and she disappeared....

I try to rationalize that I only *thought* I saw her. But it happened four times.

22. I Felt a Delicious Peace Come over Me

Joan Finch

Joan Finch is a correspondent and cat lover who lives in Langley, B.C. She read of my interest in "the mysterious" in the Langley Times *and sent me the following account of an unusual experience that involved her well-loved Persian cat, Sybby. The account is dated 24 July 1990.*

A great deal of literature has been published that alludes to the special relationship, even the kinship, that seems to exist between animal beings and human beings. There is a good deal of writing that suggests that over years of association and friendship owners and pets establish a deep and psychic interrelationship.

Nothing in Mrs. Finch's letter proves or disproves the existence of any special or psychic relationship. But the experience she writes about certainly shows how deep and meaningful the special relationship may be.

I SAW YOUR LETTER asking if anyone had had any supernatural experiences in my local newspaper. I wondered if you would be interested in a supernatural pet experience.

It happened in Toronto, in Willowdale to be exact, about twenty-eight years ago.

My husband and I were married in England four years before coming to Canada. We obtained a kitten the first year of our marriage, and after four years we were still childless. Consequently we treated our kitten, a long-haired Persian called Sybby, like a child.

I was especially attracted to Sybby, so much so that I could not come to Canada without her. We came by ship. It took us ten days to get here. The cat and I were in a cabin, sea-sick together, for those ten days.

We moved a lot after arriving in Canada. We still had no children. Sybby was about fifteen years old when we adopted our first baby. Needless to say, Sybby was very jealous of the new baby, so much so that one morning she walked out the front door, never to return.

I couldn't think what had become of her. My husband toured the district every day for weeks, thinking she may have been the victim of a car accident. I had the local children looking for her and we advertised in supermarkets, on the radio, etc., but to no avail. We even combed through a forest near us each evening, because one of the local children thought he had seen a cat that looked like the photo of Sybby in the woods.

I was very emotional about our loss and upset for about three months. If I had seen Sybby die, it wouldn't have been so bad. But I didn't know what had happened to her. Consequently she was always on my mind.

One morning as I was lying in bed, half-awake, thinking I must get up to feed our newly-adopted, four-month-old baby, I felt as though I was experiencing an electric shock. I couldn't move, my hair felt funny and all on end. Then I felt a weight jump on my stomach and it started to purr and knead me.

I wanted to see and stroke it. But we had no cat at this time. I couldn't move. Then all at once the weight leapt off into mid-air. There was no noise of anything landing on the floor. I felt a delicious peace come over me, and in that instant somehow I knew that Sybby was dead, but very happy. And from that moment on, I have never worried about her any more.

We have had a dog and lots of cats since Sybby. At the time of writing, I have four cats, but I have never been as close to any of them as I was to Sybby or had any other similar experiences.

Thank you for looking into these things.

23. The Beautiful Lady in White

M. Kirkpatrick

Mrs. M. Kirkpatrick is a resident of North Wood-stock, Ont. She was born in Chelsea, England. She read my request for true-life "ghost stories" in the Woodstock newspaper The Daily Sentinel-Review *and sent me her own account of the appearance in 1965 or 1966 of the Beautiful Lady in White. I received the hand-written letter on 25 May 1990.*

The account is interesting in two ways. Although the ghost was not seen by Mrs. Kirkpatrick, it was seen by both her young son and her adult house guest. She later learned that there was a local tradition about a wandering spirit which inhabits small stone houses or cottages, as well as the story of a suicide in her own house.

It seems that local lore buttresses local experiences. Or is it the other way round?

I ONCE RENTED A STONE HOUSE on a farm at R.R. 7, Woodstock. The house was later burnt down, but its remains are still to be seen.

I lived there with my two boys, then ten and twelve years old. They slept in separate bedrooms upstairs. We were in the house several years.

It was getting towards Christmas. My younger son told me one morning that a beautiful lady in white had come into his room the previous night and had smiled at him. This happened for a few nights in a row.

Once I had some friends stay overnight. I put one of them in my younger son's room. Nobody had mentioned his story about the beautiful lady in white, especially not me, as nobody else had seen this lady.

Anyway, the next morning our guest came down. He asked me if I had gone into his room. I said no, because I had no reason at all to go upstairs or into his room. But as he described it, this beautiful woman in white came into the room, looked at him, smiled, and then went away.

By this time I was getting "the willies." I decided to move back into town. I figured the house must be haunted and the ghost must be a beautiful lady.

It was now very near Xmas of the following year. I was about to have another child.

One day I picked up the *Sentinel Review* and read about a ghost. There was a story of "The Lady in White." Evidently she was about to marry and her future husband had built a little stone house for her. He got killed in a crash on the eve of their wedding. So she went around to all the stone houses looking for her husband. She was harmless, according to the article.

I never saw her, but my son who is now forty-two years old will swear to this day that he saw the Lady in White. My guest saw her, too, but unfortunately he is now deceased.

I found out afterwards that a man's wife left him and he hanged himself in the little stone house in which we lived.

I believe in ghosts, as I saw two myself in England. I saw the famous ghost of Dr. Phene, well known on King's Road in Chelsea, and I saw the spirit of a nun when I was a young girl. So I now believe in ghosts.

I only wish I had seen the Lady in White. I may have been able to console her. She only goes to stone houses, and whenever I see a stone house I always think of the Lady in White.

This is a true story.

24. My First Experience with Auras

Lorraine Cannon

Does the aura exist? Is there a subtle, spiritual body that envelops the gross, physical body? Is it visible, under certain circumstances, to the unaided eye? Are some people privileged to see the aura? What, if anything, does its appearance signify?

Lorraine Cannon is a woman of Irish and English background and a long-time Torontonian. In response to my query for anomalous experiences, she sent me a letter, dated 6 Aug. 1987, in which she briefly described an experience — her first experience — with an aura, an emanation of light from a living body. The event itself took place in 1966. She was in her early forties and her hsuband was a partner in a firm that specialized in management consultant work.

It was, bear in mind, the author's first experience with auras....

TWENTY OR SO YEARS AGO, my husband and I invited a guest to the Toronto Cricket, Skating and Curling Club for dinner. He was a man of thirty-four years, and he had come down from Vancouver to join my husband's firm. We asked him to meet us at the Club around six-thirty.

My husband and I were standing at the top of the stairs, a fairly long flight. When our guest arrived and started up the stairs, I could not believe my eyes. He was dressed in a navy-blue suit, white shirt, and most unusual striped tie. Emanating from his body —

shoulder to shoulder around his head — was what I can only describe as a band of grey fluff about four or five inches wide.

When he reached the top of the stairs, he was, in fact, dressed in a beige suit, beige shirt, and paisley tie. I did not say anything to my husband or our guest at the time. We enjoyed our dinner and then, about 11:00 o'clock, we drove him to the Park Plaza Hotel. He was quite excited about joining the firm.

The next morning my husband called me from the office to tell me that the man was dead. I remember telling my husband that the next time we saw him the man would be wearing a navy-blue suit, white shirt, and most unusual striped tie. He would be wearing these clothes when he was buried. And those are the clothes he wore at the Humphrey Funeral Home on Bayview Avenue.

I had mentioned my vision to my husband on the way home from the hotel. I asked him what it meant. He said that he did not know, but that so many "funny" things had happened to me, it could mean anything.

To my knowledge that was my first experience with auras. I have had a few experiences with them since then, but nothing that I can confirm.

25. Unusual Sounds in the Attic

Gladys Ramsay

I received the following letter from Mrs. Gladys Ramsay, a resident of Dashwood, Ont. She saw my letter requesting "ghost stories" in the London Free Press *and responded with this account of the haunted house she and her family owned in the 1960s.*

There is no question houses have character. A specific house may have a spirit all its own, although what is at stake is precisely how literal a meaning should be given to this statement. What Mrs. Ramsay is describing is a poltergeist.

June 8, 1990

DEAR MR. COLOMBO:

In the late sixties we lived in an old farm house outside of London, Ont. From the first week we used to hear unusual sounds in the attic. So my husband and son went up with flashlights to check it out, but they found no holes and no signs of squirrels.

The next evening the sounds from the attic were frightening, as though giant birds were bouncing off the walls. This was odd since one of the first things my husband did after we moved in was to insulate the attic. Another trip up to the attic was to no avail.

A few weeks later, around 3:00 a.m., we were awakened with the sounds of cupboard doors opening and closing. We all woke up, except for our oldest son who is a heavy sleeper. We put the lights

89

on and we went downstairs to check. Everything was fine.

We had a German shepherd named Prince at that time. He slept on a mat by the kitchen door. He was terrified. His ears were flat to his head and he never made a move or even barked. This was our watchdog! We never even locked a door while we had this dog.

One day during the fall of the year, I was staining the old staircase. I decided to make a cup of tea and went downstairs. After one cup, I put the teapot back on the stove, and climbed up the stairs and continued with my work. About an hour later I went back downstairs for another cup of tea but couldn't find the teapot. I wasn't going to let it get the better of me, so I decided I'd have a glass of milk. When I reached for the milk, there was the teapot!

After all these happenings, I talked to the man who had sold the house to us. He now lived across the road from us. I explained what had been going on and he said the previous tenants had told him pretty well the same thing had happened to them. He said the only explanation he had was that an elderly sister and brother had lived in the house for years. This was when his parents had owned it, and they told him the brother and sister had a quarrel and the sister told her brother she wouldn't speak to him for the rest of her life and when her mother and father visited them they spoke through them.

Our daughter always had the feeling of a man's presence in the house. Many a day and night we'd hear heavy footsteps on the staircase and along the upstairs hall. The minute anyone went up to see what was making the noise, it would stop.

I should mention our dog Prince always came upstairs at night to check us out. He visited our bedroom first. He would touch our hands with his nose to let us know he was there and then he went into the children's rooms. The night we heard the cupboard doors banging, he never moved. We were told animals are afraid of the unknown.

I hope you'll be able to make something out of it. Please let us know when your book will be published.

Yours truly,
Mrs. Gladys Ramsay

P.S. Sorry I couldn't mention names of previous owners and addresses. It would hurt a lot of people. The house stands empty to this day. It is so sad because my husband renovated this beautiful old home and we loved it. We sold it to a customs agent who sold it to a lawyer who rented it out. From there on we lost track of it. We heard through friends and old neighbours that it is vacant. As I said, it is a long way off the road and surrounded with trees.

26. You Would See Just a Whiteness

Fred Tiley

I received the following letter from Fred Tiley, a resident of Bradford, Ont. It was postmarked 24 May 1990.

Mr. Tiley wrote to me in response to my request, made in a local weekly newspaper, for real-life "ghost stories." Here, in minimally edited form, appears the text of his letter.

In subsequent correspondence I learned from Mr. Tiley that the house in question, which he bought in 1968 and sold in 1988, is still standing at No. 10 Pleasant Avenue, River Drive Park, a small community north on the Holland River, north of Newmarket, Ont.

SIR:

I would like to relate to you my family's experience with a ghost that made his home with us. First, some background.

We bought the house from a widow lady by the name of Mrs. Gleaves. We never met her because the house was being rented when we bought it in 1979. But Mrs. Gleaves held a one-year mortgage. She renewed the mortgage for another two years, and in all that time we never got to talk to her.

After we had lived in the house for a few years, we started to get the feeling something was going into the kitchen. Now let me explain about our ghost. The only time we saw it was at night between 8:30 and 10:00. It always went into the kitchen. At different times over the years, my ex-wife and five kids and myself saw the ghost many times.

This ghost didn't really have any shape. Sometimes you would see just a whiteness. Other times you would just sense that the ghost went into the kitchen. At different times one or another of the family members would say, "There goes the ghost."

To my knowledge, no one outside of our family saw the ghost. It was a friendly ghost and never upset anyone. But it did one thing. It used to turn our used tea cups upside down and put them on a small counter. This didn't happen too often. But it was proof to us that the ghost did exist.

After our mortgage was paid off, Mrs. Gleaves came by to see the house and all the work we had done on it. When we got talking, we told her about the ghost. That was when she told us that her hsuband died in the house and it was his habit to go into the kitchen every evening to make a cup of tea.

We sort of think the ghost was Mr. Gleaves. And the funny thing was that after Mrs. Gleaves's visit, we never saw that ghost again.

27. I Felt a Sort of Calm

Carol Betts

Carol Betts of Komoka, Ont., sent me a letter about a number of strange experiences which occurred to her almost two decades ago.

Betts was born in Toronto of Irish-English ancestry. She had no strange experiences as a child.

I received her letter on 30 May 1990 and have slightly copy edited it for presentation here.

DEAR MR. COLOMBO:

I am writing to you in response to your letter to the editor which appeared in the *London Free Press*.

First of all, I am going to tell you I am a Christian and I was a Christian at the time of my experiences. These happened many years ago when my children were little. Lorie is now twenty-two; she was about four when the first incident took place.

At the time we lived in a small house in Strathroy, Ont. My girls were put to bed in one room in the early evening. But girls being girls, even at their young age they would not go to sleep. So I put the oldest girl, Lorie, in my bed in my room. I then went into the kitchen to do the supper dishes. I was just about done when I looked into the bedroom (I could see into it from the kitchen) to make sure Lorie was sleeping.

There was a lady standing beside the bed looking down at Lorie.

She was wearing a long white dress and had blonde, wavy hair that fell just below her shoulders. She looked over at me, then she looked down at Lorie. Then she backed up and disappeared. The only thing that was behind her was the wall.

You are probably wondering if I was afraid. No, I wasn't. I felt a sort of calm. To this day I believe this lady is Lorie's Guardian Angel.

Some time after that incident I had put the girls to bed and had gone to watch T.V. They had been in bed for about one hour and everything was quiet. The girls' room was in full sight of the living-room. I always kept their door open about two inches. I don't know what made me look over that way, but I did. I saw a hand come around the door and pull it open. I got up to see which one of the girls was out of bed and playing a trick on me. I looked in the room and both girls were in bed fast asleep.

This time I was frightened. But I never saw the lady or the hand again.

The next experience I had occurred when my mother-in-law passed away. I couldn't sleep the whole night because I kept hearing her tell me to tell Richard (her youngest son) that she was all right and not to worry about her.

I think she knew that she was going to die. The night before, she called me and talked for a long time. This was very unusual for her because it was long distance and she was on a very limited budget. She told me her job was going to be the death of her. And she died the next day, running to catch a bus after finishing a day of work. I truly believe she knew something was going to happen.

The next two experiences happened at my place of work. I work in a nursing home here in Komora. I was standing in a room talking to some friends. I had my hands behind my back, and someone or something put its hand over mine. I turned around to see who it was and there was no one there.

My face went white and my friend asked me what was wrong so I told her what had happened. She said no one else came in the room. She was scared so we left.

The other thing that happened was while I was washing the dining-room floor. (I was on housekeeping at the time.) The door opened and I saw our maintenance man walk in. He had on a two-tone brown jacket which was brand new. He walked into the kitchen. Not five minutes later the same door opened again and he walked in again.

I asked him, "How did you get out of the kitchen without me seeing you?" And he said he had just got there. But he had on the same two-tone brown jacket. His wife had just given it to him for Christmas.

I know these experiences sound strange, but they all really did happen.

I haven't seen any full-body apparitions since then, but sometimes I see things move out of the corner of my eye. Or I will hear someone call my name, especially when I am in one Woolco store in London.

That reminds me, at Easter this year, I was in Woolco looking for some Easter candy. I was talking to one of the sales ladies. We were about three feet apart. An empty Easter basket came from somewhere and landed between us on the floor. We just stood and looked at each other. There were no basket displays or people right near us. So I just told her it must be the Woolco ghost!

Please excuse my writing and spelling. It is almost midnight. But I knew if I didn't take time to write to you now, I probably never would.

I am glad to be able to share these things with you. Because, being a Christian, I am not supposed to believe in things like this. But I can't help it.

I really did experience all of these happenings.

Yours truly,
Carol Betts

28. Joseph's Story

Pat Loewen

P*at Loewen, a resident of Clearbrook, B.C., was deeply moved when she read "The Death of Roger" in an earlier collection I edited called* Extraordinary Experiences. *The account was written by Kay Belanger of Port Mellon, B.C., and it told of a family tragedy that was tinged with the supernatural.*

Mrs. Loewen had a tragedy of her own, one that is suggestive of the supernatural. She sent me her account on 13 Sept. 1989 and called it "Joseph's Story." It is being published here for the first time.

"Here is a story I have written about my little brother Joseph and the events surrounding the day he died," she explained. "I hope you find it interesting."

I find it moving, and I assume other readers will as well.

JOSEPH WAS THE BABY OF THE FAMILY. Besides little Joseph the family consisted of six sisters, including me, and one brother. We all tried to help our busy dad and mom raise Joseph. He had been born on August 9, 1972. That gave the two of us a shared understanding. We were both Leos.

As he grew older, we had conversations and they often centered around what it would be like when we were dead. Our dad had taught us that if a person died quickly, without notice, the soul would become an earth-bound spirit. Not aware of its death, it would spend eternity feeling lost and lonely.

When Joseph was ten, he was diagnosed as having "a stiff heart." Cardiac specialists didn't know what to do about his condition. During one of Joseph's many medical appointments, the doctor gently explained that he didn't know how long Joseph would live.

We lived at Langenburg, Sask., and Joseph was an altar boy at our church. Understanding that his death could be close at hand or years away, he made it his business to prepare his soul to meet his God.

One evening, Dad, Mom, and Joseph were driving home from church. "Mom," Joseph said, "I'm not afraid to die, 'cept there's one part of dying I'm kinda scared of."

"What part is that, son?"

"Well, I'm scared about the part where they shove bamboo sticks under your fingernails."

"Who on earth is going to do that to you, Joseph? Where or from whom did you hear this lie?"

"I don't know. It's just the part of death I'm afraid of."

Dad and Mom laid his fear to rest.

It was on July 27th, 1984, when two of my sisters (Dorothy and Terry) and their kids came visiting from British Columbia. I was late meeting them at From's Lake Park. When I arrived, the whole family was there. All the kids were out playing in the man-made lake. It was the only swimming hole for miles so we forgave the lake its murky water. At least it didn't have too many leeches.

Mom was sitting on the beach, watching her grandchildren enjoy the water. It was so nice that her daughters from B.C. had managed to come out this summer. They arrived in time for Pat's birthday, but couldn't stay for Joseph's. So she planned this day at the lake as an early twelfth birthday celebration.

Joseph walked up to Mom, his new goggles in hand. A grin spread into a smile.

"Know what, Mom? Today's the first time in my life I ever made friends with the water. These goggles are really neat!"

Mom was very pleased. Joseph had always been afraid of the water, just like her. "That's great, Joseph! I sure am glad you're enjoying it."

"Yeah," he grinned, "water really is my friend now."

All afternoon Joseph could be seen, crawling up on the wharf, then jumping in. He went over his head in water for the first time.

Anna-Marie (Joseph's next-in-age sister) and I were sitting on the beach blanket talking with Mom and our other sisters. Joseph came up and asked us if we wanted to go swimming with him one more time. Neither of us felt like it so away he went. We watched him stand on the wharf, shaking like a leaf. Whenever he got cold, his lips would become tinged with blue and he would shake. I watched as he secured his goggles, then plunged into the deepest part of the lake.

"How remarkable!" I commented. "For a kid that's always hated the water, he sure is having a riot today."

It was five o'clock, and Mom and Dorothy had to go to the farm and prepare supper. The kids hadn't finished swimming yet so the rest of us arranged to pack up at five-thirty. The time to leave came all too soon. We called for everyone to get ready to go. Terry, Anna-Marie, and I called for Joseph. He was nowhere to be seen.

Panic spread quickly. Too quickly. Kids do just wander off sometimes. Terry phoned Mom to see if Joseph had gone home with her. He hadn't. Mom knew. She started to weep. A mother's premonition.

At the lake we were frantic. Where was he? We ran around asking if anyone there had seen him in the last while. No one had. Joseph's friends at the lake ran all over the grounds searching for him. So did many helpful adults. Anna-Marie and I went into the water. I had a feeling he was in it. At its deepest, the lake is only six feet deep. If we could find him, we could save him. Panic.

It was now five-thirty-five. We searched everywhere. Did he wander into the bushes? Look, quick! Maybe he's sick or something. Each building was searched again and again. Exasperation!

Once more the farm was phoned. Everyone there came to look for him except Dad and Mom. They needed to be alone.

A team of professional swimmers were at the lake that day, twelve in all. One by one they dove into the greenish-brown water, searching the lake bottom. They found nothing.

A family friend named Blaine and Dorothy and I decided to search the water around the wharf. We made a duck-dive to the bottom and searched the mud with hands and feet. We came up for air when our lungs were bursting and then went down again. Dorothy was a C.P.R. instructor so if she could find him she might be able to revive him. All three of us were scouring the bottom, propelling ourselves by grabbing handfuls of mud and rock.

Suddenly we shot up, three heads surfacing at the same time. I had heard a voice. So had Dorothy and Blaine at the same moment. The voice said, "What if you find him *right now*? You might touch his foot. What are you going to do?"

We had all panicked at the thought. What could we do? We couldn't handle it. We got out of the water. Whose voice was it?

There was nothing left to do but cry and pray. We set up camp on the beach right where we were and where Joseph went missing. What if he had wandered off or been kidnapped? We weren't leaving till he left with us.

Dorothy and I started a rosary. It was my turn to cry. "Joseph, where are you? Are you okay? Are you scared and lonely?" I couldn't shake the fear that he was scared. I was rocking back and forth. "Holy Mary, Mother of God..." Please God, where is he?

Was I dreaming? There he was. Joseph was standing there, his blue eyes twinkling fiercely, blond hair shining. He had on his favourite blue-and-white striped shirt. Our two family budgies were twittering on his shoulders. They had died long ago.

"Hi, Pat, why are you crying? What's your problem?"

"Joseph! Are you okay? What happened?"

"I dunno. I was standing on the wharf, and all of a sudden...ooff...it felt like someone hit me real hard on the back. I was just jumping in. Everything went black...and here I am! Boy, am I gonna have fun...This is gonna be the *best* game of hide-and-seek I've ever played!"

"Are you okay?" I cried.

"Well, what does it look like to you? Do I look sad? Hee, hee, man, is this gonna be fun! Well, take care of yourself. I'll be seeing you. Bye-bye for now, sis."

Off he went. I told Dorothy what had just happened. Did she think I was dreaming?

In all it took nineteen long hours of searching around the lake again and again. Park management left food and coffee in the main building for us. It was a long night.

No one slept. We prayed and cried, talked about Joseph, joked about him. Was he dead? Was I dreaming? Did I really see him? "Your turn to search the lake. I wouldn't want some poor sucker to bump into his body if he floated to the top!" Hysteria. Laughter. Then tears.

At noon the next day, police divers came to drag the lake. It was morbidly funny watching their flippers go up and down in perfect harmony. They flippered under the dock, then took out their dragline. We all stood together, waiting.

First time around the wharf, no Joseph. Whew! On the second round, their right arms came shooting out of the water. They had found him.

His body was no more than four feet from the dock in less than six feet of water. He was lying on his side. At least fifteen people had searched that exact spot with their hands, inch by inch. I had; so had Dorothy and Blaine. At daybreak that morning, my husband had lain on the wharf and visually inspected the settled water. He could see right to the muddy bottom. He hadn't seen Joseph.

I phoned Mom. She knew exactly where they had found him before I had a chance to tell her.

I viewed his remains for the sake of official identification. He was on his side, one leg raised, arms bent, ready to jump. His mouth was frozen in an...ooff...shape. Just like he said.

At the funeral, Mom knew Joseph was watching. He told her that it was neat that all his friends had come to say goodbye.

I still see him every now and then. So does Mom. We know he's not scared and lonely. He's happy...and waiting.

29. I Was Extremely Nervous

Brenda Silsbe

Brenda Silsbe, a resident of Terrace, B.C., sent me the account of an odd experience involving a lighthouse on Georgian Bay — with bannisters that were there and then were not there — in a letter dated 12 May 1990.

She had read my book Extraordinary Experiences *and she wanted to share with me and my readers an "extraordinary experience" that occurred to her in the company of her cousin and her uncle. To vouch for the authenticity of her narrative, Ms. Silsbe included with her account the names and addresses of her cousin Nancy and her Uncle Jim.*

Here is the relevant portion of the letter. What an odd experience to enliven a summer vacation!

IN THE SUMMER OF 1972, when I was eighteen, my sister (who was then seventeen) and I travelled to Toronto to visit our aunt, uncle, and cousins. On the weekend we went to their cottage on Georgian Bay. From this cottage we could see an island where a tall white lighthouse stood. My uncle informed me that this lighthouse was now automated. I was very interested in lighthouses — the romance and all — and badgered my uncle to take me over to the island in his motorboat so that I could see my first lighthouse close up.

Yes, he said, on Sunday afternoon, after church, we would go.

So on Sunday afternoon my Uncle Jim, my cousin Nancy (then seventeen years old), and I motored over to the island to see the lighthouse.

After pulling the boat up onto the beach and walking along by an old stone wall, we came to the lighthouse. It was a beautiful day and I was quite happy. I was amazed at the hundreds of seagulls. We looked at the foundations of what we thought were an earlier lighthouse and a house. Then we walked around to the entrance of the lighthouse. To our delight, someone had broken down the door. My uncle thought vandals had done it. That was unfortunate but it left the way open for us.

"Can we go up?" I asked my uncle. He couldn't see why not. Only Nancy was reticent because she was afraid of heights. We went inside and studied the stairs. They rose from platform to platform, solid wooden stairs.

I checked the bannisters. "Are you sure they are safe? Are you sure it will be all right?" I asked.

My uncle laughed. He was the most adventurous and uncon-cerned of any of us. He grabbed the bannisters. "See? Nothing to worry about."

So we started up. Uncle Jim went first — to blaze the way. Nancy went second because she wanted to walk up between us. And I climbed last. At first there were two bannisters to hold. But two or three flights up, there was only one bannister on the right-hand side. I remember moving my left hand over to grip the right bannister. Near the top, where the stairs were very narrow, there were no bannisters at all. Nancy had a very hard time at the top. I was nervous too and climbed on my hands and knees. When I looked down the hole, it was a long way down!

At the top of the lighthouse, we had a wonderful view of Georgian Bay. After searching for Gordon Lightfoot's Christian Island and discouraging my uncle from going out on the ledge, we started down in reverse order. I went first, Nancy second, and Uncle Jim third. We helped Nancy past the no-bannister stairs and climbed steadily down the one-bannister stairs, assuring Nancy that soon we'd be on the stairs with two bannisters.

We kept going — I was walking backwards — and when I paused to look over my shoulder and saw the door below, I couldn't believe my eyes. I stared open-mouthed at the stairs and door and realized what it means when people say their heart jumped into their mouth. We were at the bottom. And there was only one bannister!

When I told my uncle and cousin that we were at the door and there weren't two bannisters, they didn't believe me. They wouldn't believe until they saw the door themselves and the empty space where the left-hand bannister had been.

We looked and looked — for sawdust, fallen bannisters, marks that a bannister had ever been there, for alternate routes up the lighthouse, boards — anything. My mood went from delight to fear. I wanted to leave the island immediately! But my uncle was pleased that something unusual had finally happened to him. He wanted to stay and look around the foundations of the other buildings. I couldn't believe his calm! I finally convinced them to leave and all the way back to the cottage I trailed my left hand in the water. To think I had touched something that wasn't there!

Several years later I went back to the lighthouse with my uncle and cousin, but the door was locked so we couldn't get in to check on the bannisters. It was probably just as well! It was a gloomy day and I was extremely nervous!

It sounds like an insignificant thing — a disappearing bannister — but it certainly changed and moulded my philosophies and caused many of my friends to think again. It brought out many "extraordinary" stories from people who said they might not have shared one of their stories with me if I hadn't told mine first.

30. Two Out-of-Country Experiences

Jim Primeau

Jim Primeau, who lives in Brampton, Ont., is a listener to radio station Q-107. He heard me on that Toronto station's popular "Barometer" program, talking with the host Jim Carroll about the paranormal.

Primeau later phoned me and told me (as he expressed it) about his two out-of-country — not out-of-body — experiences. These happened to him and other witnesses while he was living in Goa, India. I encouraged Primeau to write or type out accounts of his experiences. On 11 May 1990, he delivered these twin accounts which he titled "This is my eye witness report of an out-of-country experience."

The accounts appear here in a slightly edited form. One does not have to journey to Goa for such experiences. But such events seem especially characteristic of India.

1.

IN THE WINTER OF 1973, in Goa, India, while sitting on a beach with a good friend from home and a friend from Stuttgart, Germany, under a sky full of stars, a light from the West started coming our way, heading east across the Indian Ocean.

It was very bright and global in dimension. We thought it was a meteorite or falling star. But as we watched its approach, suddenly, at about 45 degrees west, it stopped. Regardless of what was in our pipe, this light stopped in mid-air. The three of us watched it. It sat there for at least half a minute before shooting off in a straight line heading north.

This was another night in the life of the three of us.

2.

ONE EVENING AFTER SUPPER, while relaxing in our house on the beach and listening to the monsoon rains fall, another very unusual event took place.

Our back door came smashing open. There were five of us sharing the house. What happened, before any one of us could get up to close the door, was the fact that our star boarder, Lady, started barking. But very quickly her bark turned into a deep growl.

She leapt to attention, ears and tail straightening right out. Her eyes seemed to be transfixed on something. She stood about twenty feet from the door. Her head proceeded to follow whatever it was that was moving from the doorway, through the kitchen and back-door area, into the front sitting-room, through an interior open threshold that led into the bedroom area.

At that point the dog moved to the open threshold and maintained her stance at that place. By this time her growl was very light and low, as her head turned right, scanning the back bedroom and whatever was there.

Slowly her head followed this night-caller from the back bedroom to the front door, her head moving slowly from right to left. The front door opened partly. She whimpered, returned to the main sitting-room, and proceeded to do numerous circular turns to get comfortable. She finally settled down, her head resting on her front paws, eyes open.

We all looked at her and then at each other and had a great laugh.

31. Several Strange Things Occurred

Terry Hurst

*T*erry *Hurst, a resident of Vernon, B.C., spotted my request for "ghost stories" in the* Vernon Morning Star. *What Ms. Hurst described in her letter of 20 June 1990 is certainly an odd string of coincidences, if "coincidences" is the appropriate word to use to describe what happened to her and the "hoodoo" vessel she bought.*

ABOUT FIFTEEN YEARS AGO I purchased a boat, a fourteen-foot Marlin that had been sitting on a sales lot for months. There was a large hole near the stern, the result of an accident in which a woman had been thrown out of the boat. Her head was struck and she drowned.

My son made the repairs, we purchased a motor, and used the boat for several years for water-skiing. However, over the course of those years, several strange things occurred. The boat broke loose from its anchorage and ended up on nearby beaches so often that it became the brunt of neighbourhood jokes. It's quite likely that these incidents were the result of careless mooring, but one occurrence was so odd that I still shiver from the memory of it.

I woke up early one Sunday morning and went to the window. The night had been warm and still, and there, in the flat, calm water, my boat was standing vertical in the lake with only about three feet of its bow pointing skyward. When we investigated, we found the plugs in and the mooring doubly secured.

There was no "earthly" reason for the occurrence. (Could one, perhaps, suspect a restless spirit of attempting another escape?)

Finally I decided to sell the boat and put a classified advertisement in the local newspaper. When the paper came out, I looked for the ad, but it wasn't under "Boats for Sale" where it should have been. Only by sheer chance did I find it under "In Memoriam"! A photocopy is enclosed.

That was too much. Rather than sell the boat outright to anyone I might remotely know, I took it to a dealer in another town and traded it in on a new one.

The story, however, doesn't end there. Within a year that boat dealer went bankrupt.

32. I Will Be Well Known for My Writing

Sarah J. Clark

Sarah J. Clark of Newmarket, Ont., sent me a hand-written letter dated 26 May 1990. It was sent to me in response to my request for "extraordinary experiences" carried by the Aurora Banner & Newmarket Era. *(This weekly newspaper, by the way, was established way back in 1851.)*

Ms. Clark's letter was a long one; here I am reproducing only three sections from it. The opening section offers the reader a prediction for the year 2006, give or take a year. The other sections are of equal interest.

1.

IN 1974 I visited a tea room and saw Mr. Johnston, a very well known psychic. Everything he said has come true, except for one thing — I will be well known for my writing and will write one the best novels of all time. He said that only when I was fifty-six years old would I begin to write, which at this time seems true. Right now I'm *almost forty*. The book I'm supposed to write later on will be an autobiography titled *Up and Down the Cherry Tree*. Look it up in twenty years.

2.

Election time in late August 1984 in Newmarket, Ont. Canvassing door-to-door for the P.C.'s. Dusk, clear evening, six-thirty.

I walked up to Pickering College which I had been designated. There was no one there, it being summer season, except for one light on in the next building. I circled the main building with an eerie feeling three times. Nearing the front, I looked up at the second floor. There was a woman in black with black headdress. She was looking out of the window, obviously very sad. There was another lady walking away from the window.

As I was walking around the building the name "Mary Irwin" came into my mind over and over again. I continued my route, but several weeks later I was so bothered about the incident that I decided to go to the Museum and get information. I had learned that a gardener on the grounds had also seen her, and that she was called Phantom Mary.

At the museum, I said a few things: "Mary Irwin, two children, McCracken family, great sadness, the year 1876." The head of the museum wanted to know if I was a distant relative because of the information I had given her.

The museum head phoned me back and said, "Sarah, you won't believe this but..." She went on. "This is so incredible I can't believe it myself. I looked up the records and they said that a Mary Irwin had lived here. She had two girls, Virginia and Roberta, who died close together. Virginia died on the 27th of November, 1875, aged thirteen years; Roberta, on the 6th of January, 1876, aged four years. Two families wanted to own the house. The house was sold back and forth by two families. The year was right, too — 1876."

3.

One night my spoon and fork started to bend. I was petrified. I had heard of someone named Stephen Kaplan who was concerned with the paranormal, an acclaimed "vampirologist." I got an operator to phone Upper New York State. I did not know that he lived there, nor did I know his telephone number, as it was unlisted. In my mind I dialled Stephen Kaplan through the operator.

He answered the phone, laughingly saying, "This Is Your Life!"

"Mr. Kaplan," I replied, "help! My utensils are bending."

He asked, "Can you come here to New York and be tested for the paranormal?"

I said it was hard for me.

He said, "You could recharge a dead battery."

At this time this is what was happening. There was a cheap wall clock in the bedroom with a small battery in it. This battery had not been changed for several years. In the day you could hardly hear it, but at night, when asleep beside it, it would tick very loudly. Was it my kinetic energy that was recharging the battery of this clock?"

33. It Was Very Eerie for Both of Us

Cindy Evanoff

Cindy Evanoff quite often listens to Ed Needham's phone-in program on CFRB in Toronto. On 6 Dec. 1988 she heard Ed and the present editor discuss the supernatural and its effects on people's lives. As she had a haunted house story of her own to tell, she phoned the station and shared her experiences with the two of us and with the program's many listeners.

I remember thinking, as she recalled the events that took place in the house in Scarborough, Ont., in which she and her husband then lived, here is a case that can be investigated today. I confess I was a mite disappointed when I heard that the house in question could no longer be entered and examined because it had been demolished some years ago. But what we do have is a first-person account of what it was like to share a house with a poltergeist.

Cindy Evanoff was born in Toronto in 1952. She and her husband live in Markham, Ont., where she works as an office manager.

THE FOLLOWING is my experience while residing with my husband in a house at 624 Birchmount Road in Scarborough, Ontario, in 1973. The house was an old, two-storey, wood-frame, shingled affair nestled on a corner lot across from Pine Hill Cemetery. It was a very serene setting. Looking out the kitchen window, the view was of the cemetery's tall trees and the pretty flowers on the graves.

112

We lived there for two years. It should be noted that the house has since been torn down, and ten new homes have been built on the property.

In 1972, my husband was renting the house and occupying it with two other bachelors who moved out in mid-1973. At that time strange things were occurring. The mailman brought mail addressed to eight or ten different people who had, obviously, lived in the house in the past. Prior to my moving in, my girlfriend and I — now my sister-in-law — were living together elsewhere. We did not have enough money to buy end-tables for our living-room, so one night we took two large boxes over to the house to spray-paint them in the basement. I painted them on three sides and returned the next night to pick them up. I went downstairs to fetch them and I found both of them upside down with the unpainted sides showing. My husband — at that time my boyfriend — assured me that no one had been in the basement since the night before.

I was always puzzled as to why these boxes had been tampered with, especially as the painted sides were not smeared. Therefore, the paint had dried before they were turned over. There was always a feeling of someone being there in the basement.

Once when my husband was going down the stairs to the basement, he felt something grab his leg from behind the open staircase, and fell down the stairs. His shoulder still aches from time to time, even now, fifteen years later. That was the only occasion when "something" physically hurt someone in the house.

After I moved in, in 1973, a number of unexplained things happened. We had two cats who would not go upstairs to the two bedrooms. On a number of occasions, they would sit at the bottom of the stairs and look up and meow strangely from the bottoms of their throats as if they were scared to death. We had a machete that sat on the windowsill at the bottom of the staircase. Every morning for a number of weeks the machete was on the floor below the window. I would pick it up and put it back on the windowsill. But every morning it was back on the floor. I cannot remember what happened to it. One day it was gone.

Whenever we went out at night for the evening, we would turn on the porch light when we left. As soon as we got in the car to leave, the light would go off and then on again. One time we forgot to turn on the light. When my husband went to unlock the door to switch on the light, it turned on by itself. It was as though someone was saying, "Here, let me do it for you, just leave!"

On two occasions, as we pulled out of the driveway, we both saw a vision in the upstairs bedroom window. It was very eerie for both of us. When we were in the house, we never saw anything or anybody. On numerous occasions when we returned home, we heard the barbells, which my husband kept in the upstairs bedroom, clanging, as though someone was lifting and lowering them. When we went to check it out, they were on the floor as though they hadn't even been touched.

One night when my husband was out with his buddies for the evening, I stayed home and went to bed early. Our bedroom was on the main floor and beside the door to the basement. I had fallen asleep, but suddenly I woke up. The bedroom door was open and I could look out the doorway. I could see that the door to the basement was open. Who had opened it? We always kept it shut and even had a lock on the outside of the door. When I got up to close it, the door closed by itself before I could reach it. It was as though whoever lived there with us was trying to scare us into leaving.

Needless to say, I took off to the lounge of a nearby hotel where I knew I would find my sister-in-law. I told her what had happened. Some of our friends were sitting there and, of course, they cracked up laughing. We explained that things like this happened regularly in the house. I invited three or four of these people to come back to the house and they did. It was unbelievable. We were only in the house a couple of minutes when the barbells started to clang. You have never seen anything like it. These people literally looked like they had seen a ghost. Their faces drained and were totally white. After that they never joked about what was happening on Birchmount Road. I guess the only thing that kept us in that house and out of an apartment elsewhere was the rent. It was cheaper living there than it would have been to rent an apartment.

We very rarely went down to the basement, as it was not furnished and we just kept odds and ends in storage there. But several times the light in the basement went on by itself, and we would turn it off. The next time it would be on again. We did not have wiring problems as far as we knew. The other lights in the house did not go on and off like the basement light and the porch light.

Some time after these experiences occurred, we spent the evening in a neighbour's house. A woman was there who had lived for years down the street on Birchmount. She heard our story and told us that several years earlier a woman had lived in that house with her two children. The woman had gone crazy. Apparently she killed and dismembered her two children, threw them in the creek that ran behind the house, and then hanged herself in the upstairs closet. The closet was in the hall outside the bedroom where the barbells were located and where the cats refused to go.

By 1975 we had saved enough money to buy our own house. When we had packed up and were ready to move from Birchmount, my husband said he felt a pat on the back as he was getting into the truck. There was no one behind him. It was as though someone was saying, "Thanks for dropping in!"

We have a friend who is intrigued with the supernatural, etc. After talking to the management that owned the house, they agreed to let her move in. She advised us that she did not experience anything unusual. However, her daughter slept in the upstairs bedroom where our barbells were kept. The mother said her daughter felt uneasy sleeping in that room, and many a night she would not get to sleep at all. The mother said too that her cat and dog, like our two cats, would not go upstairs to the second floor!

34. A Very Special Memory
Paul McLaughlin

Paul McLaughlin is an instructor in the School of Journalism at Ryerson Polytechnical Institute in Toronto. He is the author of many articles and one of them, "Guest Appearances," appeared in the May 1990 issue of Cottage Life. *It gathered together a number of mysterious occurrences reported from Ontario's Muskoka district.*

As it happened, the same magazine ran my request for "ghost stories." Seeing my letter, McLaughlin wrote to me on 23 July 1990. In his he letter recalled an odd and unusual experience of his own. The occurrence he describes is a coincidence. Or is it?

IN 1976 I took several months off from my job as a producer at CBC Radio in Ottawa to travel in Europe. During my exploration of Greece, I became friends with a young Scottish couple (the young man, whose last name was MacAskill, believed he was a direct descendant of the Nova Scotia giant Angus MacAskill), while on the island of Ios. When I told them I'd be visiting Scotland (where I was born) in a couple of months, they urged me to look them up in Edinburgh.

Circumstances kept me away from Edinburgh. However, I was on the Isle of Skye on a typically cold and windy September evening when a strange event connected me with them. I had gone to a pub some distance from my bed and breakfast and decided to hitchhike back rather than endure a long and unpleasant walk. As you can imagine, there were few cars on the road at that time of night on the remote island. I had just about given up hope when a vehicle came along, stopped, and picked me up.

In front were a young Scottish couple. After a few minutes of exchanging biographical information, I said to the woman — whom I had been looking at quite intently — that there was something about her, a feeling as much as her looks, that reminded me of a woman I had met in Greece some months back. I told her the woman's name and said, "Is there any chance you're her sister?"

"No, I'm not," she replied. "I'm her best friend. I've known her all my life."

Although this is not an exceptionally paranormal experience, it remains a very special memory for me.

35. And Yet It Seems So Unreal

Annemarie Landry

The following letter was sent to me by Annemarie Landry, a resident of Rigaud, Que. It was dated 27 June 1990. She wrote the letter in response to my request for "ghost stories" which appeared in 1ère Édition du Sud-Ouest.

It is amazing how one cannot forget a visual event or experience like the one described by Ms. Landry. It persists in memory and remains a puzzlement for more than a dozen years — and will no doubt continue to do so for the rest of her life.

I READ YOUR LETTER in a recent edition of one of our local newspapers and would like to share with you an experience I had approximately twelve years ago. At the time I was twenty-five years old and had two children, a girl aged two and a boy just under four years of age. I was living in a very old farm house. (I was told it was 135 years old at the time.)

One night my daughter woke up crying. I got up, turned on the light in my bedroom, and went across the hall to her. She calmed down and I put her back in bed after a few minutes. I went back to my room and turned around to turn off the light.

At the far end of my bedroom, a large, egg-shaped, glowing object floated into my room. It appeared to be three or four feet in height and was floating approximately eighteen inches off the floor. It was radiating a strong golden-coloured light. The only

118

thing I can compare it to is the way a sparkler seems to shoot off rays of light.

My first reaction was to assume it was the effect of looking at my bedroom light after having been in the dark. I shifted my gaze, but the glowing light did not move with my gaze. I stood and blinked and looked for a minute.

I was nervous, but I did not think to wake my husband. For some reason I just had the feeling I should turn off the light, go to bed, and everything would be O.K. So I did and fell asleep again very quickly.

Even now, when I think about this incident, I know what I saw and yet it still seems so unreal.

I hope my story can be of some use to you. If you have any questions or anything, please feel free to get in touch with me.

36. There Really Are Ghosts

Michele L. Marshall

*T*he memoir that follows is a highly detailed account
of a haunting. The reader of Michele L. Marshall's letter will revel
in the family detail. What is missing is any sense of the identity of
the ghost, its relationship with the trapdoor that leads to the attic,
and its purpose in haunting this house. Yet the account is so
immediate! Mrs. Marshall is currently a resident of Spencerville,
Ont.

May 25, 1990

DEAR MR. COLOMBO:

My twin sons are outside on their four-wheelers so I have some
time to write to you without having to explain this letter. What I'm
about to tell you few people know except for my children and their
father.

I am thirty-nine years old, I work in a factory, and I have a home
in the country. I am the mother of four children — two are gone
and two are at home. This experience happened to me many years
ago, but it comes back to me in my mind quite often.

In December of 1978 my husband and I bought a brick home in
Prescott, Ont. We moved in shortly after Christmas. It was an
average home. It has three bedrooms and was actually built by
someone in my husband's family about one hundred years ago. I
found this out after I started searching for answers.

At the time we moved in, the children were all pretty small. My daughter had one bedroom, the three boys another, and my husband and I, the third. In my daughter's bedroom there was a closet and in this closet a set of steep stairs which lead up to the attic. When we moved in I went up the stairs and with my husband's help we lifted the trapdoor. It weighed, I'd say, about fifty pounds, and it had to be pushed straight up and over to get into the attic. To my dismay, the attic was filled with old junk. I never really got back up there. It was dark. There was no light or electricity. And I told the children never to go up the stairs. They couldn't lift the trapdoor anyway.

About two months after we moved in, I was upstairs in my daughter's room cleaning up. My daughter used the stairs to the attic to store her shoes and boots and some discarded stuffed animals and stuff. I opened her closet to put something away. It was so cold! I looked up the stairs. It was as dark as ever because there was no electric light in her closet. The trapdoor was wide open. So I moved her things away and climbed up the stairs and pulled the door back down. I was so mad! Here it was in the middle of winter and those damn kids had opened that door. I didn't know how they had done it, but they were gonna get it when they got home from school.

Now, the twins were about a year and a half old, so I blamed the two older kids, who at the time were eight and six years old. Well, it slipped my mind with my busy life, and I never did ask them about it.

A couple of weeks went by and I was in my daughter's room again, cleaning up, and I found it so cold. I thought maybe the window could use some caulking. But her closet door was ajar and I went over to close it, and it seemed like a wind was coming from the closet. So I opened it up and looked up the stairs. Well, that stupid door was open again! This was it! Those kids were getting it tonight! So when they came home from school, I lit into them, telling them about the cost of heat. This was happening during the oil embargo, and we couldn't afford to heat an uninsulated attic!

Well, they swore they had never opened that door. I looked at their faces and I could tell they were scared. So when my husband came home from work, I asked him if he had been up in the attic and he said he hadn't. I mentioned to him that I had to shut the trapdoor twice since we had moved in.

Not long after that in the spring, we bought a bloodhound, a beautiful dog whose name was Bones because he was just skin and bones when we bought him. Bones slept on a rug in our bedroom right beside me. Sometimes he would get up and check out all the kids, then come back, sniff me, lie back down.

In August it was so hot we had an air conditioner upstairs. I went into my daughter's room and threw some stuff in her closet and just automatically looked up. Sure enough that trapdoor was open again! I was so mad. Here I was trying to cool the house down and someone had left that door open, letting in all the hot air from the attic! So I went up and closed it. I remember hurting my back doing so because the trapdoor was so heavy. Well, I went out to find the kids and they said they never went near the attic. I'd had enough, so when my husband came home, I had him *nail* that door shut. He used those big four- or five-inch nails. Those little brats wouldn't get in there any more!

At the time my husband and I owned a restaurant-motel and we were spending a lot of time at work. Needless to say, we weren't getting a lot of sleep, especially as the children were so young. What I'm about to tell you now just sent chills through me...even after all these years!One evening my husband and I went to bed about 1:00 a.m. As usual, Bones was beside me. Well, he kept getting up and going out into the hall. So I got up and asked, "Is something wrong, Bones?" I thought one of the kids had fallen out of bed and was on the floor so I checked all the children. They were fine. I said, "You gotta go outside?" I started down the stairs, but he just lay down. So I went back to bed, but Bones stayed out in the hall. I said, "Come here, Bones. I'll pet you for a while." I could do this while I lay in bed. But he wouldn't come back into the bedroom. Eventually I fell asleep.

A little while later I heard my dresser drawer next to my bed being opened. I thought it was the dog. I opened my eyes and there was *this guy* going through my underwear. He was bent over and when I started to say something, he held his finger to his lips to tell me to be quiet. He was smiling. Slowly he removed his hand from my underwear, closed the drawer, stood up, turned, and walked out of the bedroom.

I lay there, stiff, my heart pounding, a tear coming to my eye. Was I going crazy? I got up about five minutes later. But it seemed like eternity before I could move. Bones was downstairs. Now he never went downstairs at night. I checked the children. All were fine. Okay, what should I do? I need sleep. I was exhausted. I went back to bed, moved real close to my husband, hugged him, and slowly went to sleep.

At this point I have to tell you what *this guy* looked like. He was about twenty-two with blond, curly hair. He had the prettiest blue eyes. I'd never seen eyes so blue as his. He had beautiful teeth. He wore a striped, blue-and-red shirt and he had sneakers on and jeans. I will never forget what he looked like or what he wore. Never.

The next day, when I was alone with my husband, I told him about the ghost I had seen. I thought he would laugh at me or tell me I was crazy. He just said, "We really need to take some time off from work." He asked if I felt threatened by the ghost. "No," I said, "it was like he was talking to me but his lips never moved." We talked about half an hour, and then we went to work.

Three days later I was upstairs cleaning up and went into my daughter's closet. You guessed it. That trapdoor was open again. How could that be? It was nailed shut. I went up and closed the trapdoor. There were no nails! None. Not even a single nail-hole. I shook I was so scared. But I didn't say anything to the kids. I went to our local library, got all sorts of books about ghosts.

What to do? Are they bad? Will they harm my children? I couldn't tell anyone about what was happening. I was afraid they wouldn't believe me, and it's such a small town. It would be all over town in no time. I kept it to myself. But I told my husband about the trapdoor to the attic. He went up and drove about fifty nails into the door. He said no one would ever get in or out of that trapdoor again!

I wouldn't undress in my bedroom because I felt someone was watching me and laughing. I dressed and undressed quickly in the bathroom. Bones wouldn't sleep upstairs any more. He slept at the bottom of the staircase. The kids asked why Bones wouldn't come upstairs any more. I just said he probably was more comfortable downstairs because it was cooler.

About five days went by. One day my husband and I came home from work about 11:00 p.m. We hadn't cashed up. We were very tired. Then our bartender called and said there was quite a bit of money in the till and did we want him to put the money somewhere. My husband said no, he would drive back and pick the money up. He told me to go to bed, he'd be home soon. I undressed in the bathroom but wouldn't go to bed without him. I was afraid and called the restaurant and asked him how long he was going to be because I couldn't go to bed without him. He said he'd be home in twenty minutes. I turned on all the lights in the house. The kids were asleep and I sat on the couch in the living-room. I turned on the stereo real low so I wouldn't wake anyone.

I heard someone coming down the stairs. I thought it was one of the twins. I looked up and there "he" was again. He was leaning over the bannister, smiling at me. He slowly walked down the stairs, never taking his eyes off me. When he got to the bottom of the stairs, he disappeared.

I slowly got up, went to the phone, and called my husband. I said, "Whatever you're doing, it doesn't matter, just come home right now! I need you! Hear? Right now!" He was home in seven minutes, and I collapsed in his arms. I said, "I can't take it any more. We have to move. I'm afraid." He argued. He said we would talk about it in the morning.

I stayed home the next day and read those books from the library. The consensus was that ghosts will not harm you. They are trapped, trapped because of dying too soon, before they could finish something. Either that or they were murdered.

I went to the people we bought the house from and asked them questions without telling them anything. Had anything ever happened while they were living in the house? No, they said. Any problems with the attic door? No. "Who owned the house before you did?" They listed the previous owners and I went through the list. No one died while living in the house. No one was ever murdered in it. Dead end.

Okay, try this. In one of the books it said that if you asked the ghost to leave you alone because he was upsetting you and scaring you, he would go away. Okay, I'll try that.

About a week went by. I was in a hurry to change my clothes and I was undressing in my bedroom. I knew he was behind me. I could feel his eyes on me. I didn't turn around. I started to cry but I said, "Please, you're scaring me. I can't live here any more if you are here too. I hold nothing against you, but I'm not strong enough to take this. So would you please leave?"

I was shaking. My heart was pounding. I heard a faint sigh, "Yes, I'm sorry." And that was the last I saw of him and the last I saw of the trapdoor opening.

Seven months later we sold the house to a young couple. After we moved to another house, I told the children about the ghost. They were fascinated, but I know they would have been scared had I told them about it while we lived there.

A couple of years later the children went "trick or treating" to that house and told the young couple living there that they had seen a ghost. They laughed and thought the kids were trying to scare them. If only they really knew the truth!

I have shared this with you because I want the world to know that, yes, there *really* are ghosts. They do exist. I will never forget my experience. My children believe me and they have an open mind compared with mine at their age.

What bothers me today, so many years later, is why *he* was so happy. I thought ghosts were supposed to be sad. Why was he always smiling? Why did he make me feel like he meant me no harm? Why was he in that house? If I went back there, would I see him again? If I had stayed, would he have talked to me?

Sincerely,
Michele L. Marshall

37. Something Else Was Living There

Dan Carter

Dan Carter is a Torontonian who heard me being interviewed by Bill Carroll, host of "Barometer," the popular early afternoon program on radio station Q-107. Phoning me at my home later that day, he shared with me the story of a spate of poltergeist-like disturbances that he and other members of his family experienced in their apartment. (For the record, the apartment is No. 704, 3 Glamorgan Avenue, Scarborough, Ont.)

What Dan Carter described could be called the effects created by a poltergeist, a "noisy ghost." A poltergeist is known by its effects, not by its appearance, although at the end of this account "something" does appear. Dan Carter accepted my invitation to write out a sequential account of his experiences. I received it on 17 April 1990 and here, in a minimally edited form, it is.

A SERIES OF EVENTS made our lives rather interesting over a period of from six to eight months.

On October 1st, my brother and I rented an apartment in Scarborough, off Kennedy Road, near Highway 401. From the time we moved in, odd things would happen. They occurred during our absences from the apartment; e.g., I would come home from work and find all the doors inside the apartment closed, the doors to the bedroom and bathroom, etc. Sometimes lights would be on when I entered and then a short time later they would go off by themselves. My brother and I kept blaming each other for these occurrences.

The linen closet at the end of the hall was extremely cold. We used to keep milk in it as it was colder than the fridge.

We were the first tenants in this apartment for it was a new building.

Sometimes my fiancée, who worked right across the street, would come to the apartment for lunch. One day when we were out, she came over and found the hall light on and every tap in the place on full blast. Thinking it odd, she shut the taps off — the kitchen tap, the taps in the bathroom sink, the tub and shower taps, etc. That evening she asked us why we had left them on.

One night my fiancée and I were watching T.V. in the living-room. There was a loud crash in the kitchen. From the kitchen a cigarette butt flew through the air at great speed and smashed into the back of the front door of the apartment, leaving a black mark from its ash on the top part of the door. I would guess the distance to be about ten or twelve feet. When I went into the kitchen to clean up the mess, I found that nothing was disturbed.

Sometimes bedroom doors would close, either one at a time or all at once, with great force. One time I came home early from work. As I got off the elevator, I heard music playing, very loud music. As I approached the apartment, I discovered the music was coming from inside. To be sure, I checked the apartments next to mine, above and below, by placing my ear to their doors. The music was definitely coming from my apartment. It occurred to me that my brother had come home from work early and was playing music. I was going to give him a blast for playing the music so loud. When I opened the door to the apartment, everything went dead quiet. My brother was not at home. The only stereo in the apartment was located in his room. It was not on.

When I got married, my wife, my brother, and I stayed in the apartment. Once, she and her girlfriend were preparing to hold a Tupperware party and were cleaning up. When they were doing the dishes, they placed the glasses upside down on the drainboard. The glasses kept flipping right-side up. They did not fall over, but went up in the air, turned over, and landed right-side up. This event was witnessed by three people. They phoned me and said, "Come home now. We will meet you in the lobby." When I got there fifteen minutes later, the girls were in the lobby, white and hysterical. To make matters worse — when they took the elevator from the seventh floor down to the lobby, the elevator went back up to the seventh floor, stopped there, came back down, stopped, and nobody got off.

The Tupperware party was held that evening. All the people who entered the apartment that night reported the same thing occurring. Their watches stopped. If they stepped outside the apartment and into the hall, their watches would go again. Re-entering, they would stop again.

We finally decided that there was something else living there with us. We also knew that it was out and about because you could hear the breaking of glass. It sounded like expensive crystal. Suddenly the room would get extremely cold, as cold as the linen closet. We believe it lived in the closet.

At night, when you were in bed but not yet asleep, you could hear the chains on the living-room lamps clang against the stems of the lamps. Going out to check on these noises, you could hear them more clearly. But as soon as you entered the living-room, they would stop. All the while the windows were closed.

Sometimes, at night, my wife would wake me up and say, "Someone is walking down the hall." Listening, I would tell her it was my brother and he was playing a joke on us. Getting out of bed and listening by the door, I heard something walk past, stepping with one foot and dragging the other, walking towards the linen closet. Opening the door very gently, and jumping out to surprise my brother, I was surprised to find no one there. My brother's door was closed tightly. It was warped. You had to body-slam it to close it tight.

In March of 1974, I received a call informing me my grandmother had died. My mother and father flew up from Miami for the funeral. My father stayed with his family, my mother stayed with us. We told my mother not to worry about the odd noises. Apartments are noisy places, we told her.

The next morning my mother informed us she was leaving. When we asked her why, she told us she was lying on the sofa, almost asleep, when she heard glass break in the dining-room. Suddenly the room got extremely cold. Reaching for a blanket, something touched her on the shoulder, as if to say, "It's okay. It's only me." She said it was a very warm, loving touch. But she never forgot it.

That night she decided to prove to herself that something did, indeed, live with us. My mother stood a cigarette on its end on top of the T.V. set. Sitting on the sofa with my brother and his girlfriend, she spoke. "If there is anything in this room, prove it to me by knocking my cigarette down." The cigarette fell down. My mother then stood the cigarette up again and said, "A kid can do that. I want you to really prove it." The cigarette then flew across the room as if someone had swatted it. My mother was convinced.

Somehow word got out about our place, and people would come to the door asking, "Is this the apartment with the ghost? Can we see it? Would you like to sublet it?"

The last thing I remember of "the ghost" was this. I was asleep when, all of a sudden, it was cold in the bedroom, so cold that I woke up shivering. I looked toward the doorway. It was wide open and a dark shadow entered the room. I felt frozen and could hardly move. The only thing I could do was close my eyes and shiver. Then the room warmed up and it, whatever it was, was gone.

These events took place sixteen years ago. If you need further information, call me or my wife Debbie.

38. I Am a Firm Believer

Sharon Shields

*The following letter was received on 14 June 1990
from Sharon Shields who is a resident of Ajax, Ont. It was written
in response to my request for "ghost stories." I am reproducing the
letter in the author's own words, except for some copy editing.*

*The letter suggests that the author is a natural-born psychic. It
may be that as a child she was contacted by the spirit which Roman
Catholics and others refer to as one's "guardian angel."*

*Anyway, the author is of Celtic background and, as everyone
knows, such people are believed to be naturally psychic.*

I HAVE BEEN TOLD you are looking for true supernatural facts to
write in your book. I must admit I had to give this a lot of thought
before writing as I feel my experiences are very sacred to me. But it
is a fact that people teach people by sharing their knowledge or
experience of knowledge.

I am a firm believer in the existing energies and spiritual dimensions that we live with. In fact, it has taken me from childhood to
where I am now, trying to keep in tune with the spirit within. This
is now my living. To try to fulfil my purpose by sharing the gifts I
have been given, by helping those people who are in need of
whatever assistance I can give them to direct their pathways. In
fact, I have some very dear friends who dedicate themselves to

helping others. The search is becoming more clear to many people who are realizing that life is not just in the natural existence of shopping malls, new cars, or big homes. We all are part of it, sometimes we get lost in it, even I have; but to realize it and recognize our spirit needs, to live for our real purposes, whatever they may be, is where the real fulfilment and happiness lie.

My first experience was, as I recall, when I was about six years old. We lived at the end of town in Huntsville, Ont. My sister, a friend, and I went up the hill into the bushy area where there was a small clearing with a big rock to the right under a large tree. We heard a noise and a big dog came barking out from behind the tree. He didn't seem to notice me and chased after my older sister and her friend, who took off screaming, forgetting me. I was so frightened I just stood there. The dog stood at the edge of the clearing, barking, looking at them, still not seeming to notice me. I climbed up on the rock, wondering whether or not to run the other way, when I heard a lady's voice say, "Don't be afraid, Sharon, he won't harm you; he was only meant to frighten them away so I could talk to you."

I was startled, as I had not seen this woman, I had not seen her or heard her come, she was just there. She told me she had a message for me. I don't remember everything she said, but I've always remembered this: "Sharon, you have a purpose to fulfil, your path will be different from most others, so you must remember this: When you are hurt, as you will be many times, you must never be vengeful, you must forgive and turn the other cheek, because you will always be protected from great harm. You must also remember never to speak against anyone in a lie. If you must say how you feel, speak the truth, but even then it's best not to, unless it is nice, no matter how you feel or what they do to you, as it won't matter if others do this, but you can't, you won't be able to, or you will suffer until you learn; it is very important to remember this, as your purpose is of a different order." I couldn't speak for a moment. Then I asked her who she was and where she came from. She said I would know in time. The dog had been quiet while she spoke and still never looked at me. It seemed as though everything had become still, nothing moved.

I looked at her face, but yet I don't seem to recall seeing it clearly.

Her eyes were light, yet she didn't and did look into mine. Then she was gone, just gone. She came as an old woman, a cane in one hand, no, I should say like a long stick. She had an old, large-brimmed hat on, an old, large, brown bag over her shoulder, and layers of old patched clothing on. I never saw anyone dressed like that, or like her, before or after.

I did make a few errors through my earlier life with my temper, when someone was being unkind or untruthful, but I did learn it always hurt me more to feel vindictive or angry. I started to see her image very clearly, and many times I have been protected before someone hurt me by warnings I received very strongly.

My friends now are good people who have travelled a lot of roads similar to mine. It was no coincidence, the time was right.

But as I grew up, many times things took place whereby I learned that there are many things that cannot always be proved but do exist, and it is a real enlightenment to know how much we all are a part of it and how wonderful it can make our lives. My dreams are not always normal outlets of obscure pictures and fears or tensions, but some dreams are very real and do predict things before they happen. You have to know that these particular dreams are a way of letting your own inner consciousness guide you, warn you, or help you. They are vivid, clear, detailed dreams. Learning the difference between them is very important. To accept the fact that there are realities that do exist, to some of us stronger than others, but accepting them and knowing the difference between imagination and the fact that they exist, can benefit a person greatly.

A lot of these realizations can be looked at very scientifically.

The Radiance Technique of healing through energies that can pass through our bodies, as our bodies consist of energy, is a very ancient and real form of medicine. Not only of body, but also of mind. From intelligent cultures, as some people like to feel theirs is, to cultures that to others seem ignorant, all have worked with ancient teachings passed on to help and cure others. It seems only the pretenders get on the media, and people pass by the reality of the seen facts in evidence, because they are afraid of receiving ridicule and their analytical minds will not allow them to accept what they can see.

I have from time to time in my life been connected with spiritual beings, who have given me information or who have simply shown themselves to me, not always from this time. It is unique and hard to explain.

Clairaudience, to hear voices, I have experienced. Clairsentience, to identify through the senses of smell, odours, too. Clairvoyance, to see beyond time and space as we know it in our daily frame of time and space, I have worked with. I know many good, intelligent, sane, educated people who work in normal careers as well as in all these fields, who experience and work with the spiritual essences of these connections to help others and to learn themselves.

A few times in my life, in times of crises, I have had a wolf appear in front of me to show me that this situation or that person was dangerous and to remove him from my path. The first time this wolf appeared, it frightened me so terribly! I thought my heart would stop. Later, a few times I wondered, why does it always come so frighteningly, but I realized I wasn't listening to my own voice inside, nor was I heeding any warnings, so I had to be shocked into listening. It was certainly effective as a warning.

The first wolf appeared when I was dating someone. I realized his moods were very changeable and he was an extremely possessive and jealous person, yet I tended to make excuses. I turned around one day and looked into this person's face. I looked into a black wolf's face, with teeth bared and burning red eyes. The fear nearly killed me. I couldn't move. Finally I turned away, telling myself I was imagining this. I looked back, it was still there. I never spoke, but I quickly left the room.

A little time later I tried to tell this person he had to stop seeing me. I had left it for too long. He seemed calm, understanding, and accepting, but he wanted to stay a little longer. Mistake! I felt something was different in the house, but my mind was running in too many directions to focus. The house suddenly was ice-cold, a lady's voice kept calling, "Sharon, get out of this house, get out now." I was confused and not sure of what to do. She called again, "Get out of the house, he's going to kill you."

All the dogs in the neighbourhood started to bark. The house was so cold I saw my breath in the air. My two children both woke up screaming at the same time. Suddenly I couldn't move. Then I ran into their room and grabbed them. He was behind me, trying not to show the anger, saying, "Put them back to bed, they only had a nightmare, the heat will come back on."

I chose my words carefully as I moved, calmly explaining, "The heat won't work. Probably the furnace was broken, too cold. My parents were living not far away, we'll go for a while, you can come."

I hurried out, terrified inside that I might not make it, praying to God to help us. We got there; he came. My parents knew instantly something unusual had happened. They had not been able to sleep and had thought of me. I stayed with them until the situation was under control. Things turned out fine. But the next morning, I went back to the house and into the living-room. By the couch, under the cushion he sat on, I found a loaded gun. So thankful I am.

Believe me, knowing how so many people block out their own experiences of the supernatural (as it is called by many), and knowing how many choose to remain skeptical and ignorant of the spiritual realities that exist, it is a different area to release to the public view.

39. A Lady Ghost Who Walks

Linda C. Marlok

The sadness of the human condition is as much the subject of the experience that follows as is the supernatural.

Parapsychologists have long noted that times of grief are times productive of psychical phenomena. Indeed, for some people, the two seem to be inseparable.

Certainly it is a time of grief that is being recalled in this letter sent to me by Linda C. Marlok, a housewife for twenty years and a mother of three and now a resident of Val Caron, Ont.

12 July, 1990

DEAR SIR,

I read your letter in the *Northern Life* newspaper in Sudbury, Ont., the one asking people to write to you about happenings and sightings of ghosts, UFOs, and strange creatures.

The story I'm writing to you about is true.

The incident was something that happened to me about six years after my father died. Members of my family and I decided to go to visit my mother for the weekend. At the time she was staying at the cottage that had been my father's favourite place. It was a log cabin up on a hill which overlooks a small lake called Bat Lake, at Minden, Ont.

Our first night at the cottage I was awakened shortly after going to bed. I could hear footsteps pacing up and down the hallway. I thought it was my mother so I got up to go and make sure. No one was there. Everyone was in bed sleeping. I found it strange so when I went back to bed, I woke up my husband and told him of the strange sounds.

The following day I spoke with my mother about what had happened that night. She replied, "Oh, yes, I have a lady ghost who walks the hallway at nights. It's nothing unusual. You see, the lady who was the former owner had died in this cottage, and she walks the hallway at nights. It was her sister who sold us the cottage and who told us of this back then."

Later that day my mother and I exchanged harsh words, and I went to the washroom crying. I said the following words in my upset state: "Dad, I'm sorry, I can't reason with her, and I don't know what to do. I find it hard to hold my promise to you."

Just then, under my feet, there were three knocks on the floor boards. I could feel the vibration and so frightened was I that I left the cottage right away.

There is no basement to the cottage, just a crawl space, and the door to it is always padlocked. It was so when I went to check.

There are other incidents that have happened to my sister, my brother-in-law, and many other people who have stayed at this cottage.

Sincerely,
Linda C. Marlok

40. I Had Heard of Astral Projection

Barry Brown

Barry Brown is a commentator on current affairs who specializes in writing articles and columns about social and political developments in Canada for readers throughout North America. He was born in Toronto, and since 1981 his byline has appeared in over seventy publications in Canada and the United States. One of the articles he wrote for the Buffalo News *was nominated for a Pulitzer Prize in 1989.*

On 4 Jan. 1990, Brown sent me the following account of an experience with "astral projection." The phenomenon of "astral projection" is also known as "double-going." The event or experience described by Brown occurred in 1960. It is his sole paradoxical experience — to date.

I WAS SIXTEEN AT THE TIME. One night, as I was lying in my bed dozing off to sleep, I suddenly found myself outside my parents' house, in the alleyway between my house on Gardiner Road and the apartment building that faced Eglinton Avenue. I was in a blue, almost amorphous body, but with legs and arms and, I suppose, a head.

I had heard of astral projection and my first thoughts were, "Hey, I've astral projected." I decided to test this out by walking to my (then) girlfriend's home. With very long strides, I walked through the alley, across Eglinton, past Forest Hill Collegiate, to the apartment building where she lived. All this time, I took great care to observe the scenery around me and make sure it all looked real and this wasn't a dream.

Standing outside her apartment building on Bathurst Street, I wondered how I would get in. Suddenly, there I was, in her bedroom. Now, although I had visited her parents' apartment, I had never been in her bedroom. But I saw her grandmother sleeping in a bed by the window and my girlfriend, Laura, also sleeping in a bed by the door. This was also curious, for while I had met Laura's grandmother, I didn't know she lived there.

I stood beside Laura. Her brow was furrowed as if she was having a bad dream. Then, as she stirred as if to wake up, I abruptly found myself back in my own bed. I checked the clock for the time.

The next day, I met Laura and told her I had astral projected to her home the night before. "Sure," she said.

"You sleep in a bed by the door, don't you, and your grandmother sleeps in your room in a bed by the window?"

"Yes," she said, "how did you know?"

"I told you, I astral projected. You looked like you were having a bad dream."

"I have a bad dream every night," she said, then added, "What time were you there?"

"Midnight, give or take a few minutes."

"I woke up at midnight," she said, "because I thought someone was there."

"That's it."

41. The Haunting of McKay Avenue School

Ron Hlady

Haunted houses in Canada are legion. (Or at least reports of haunted houses are legion.) Haunted primary or secondary schools are few and far between. But here is one....

Ron Hlady is a Building Preservation Technician with the Edmonton Public Schools Archives and Museum. He wrote this account of his experiences in the building in which he works. "The Haunting of McKay Avenue School" originally appeared on a page reserved for "ghost stories" in the Edmonton Journal, *30 Oct. 1988.*

I DON'T LIVE IN A HAUNTED HOUSE but I do work in a haunted school.

McKay Avenue School is the Museum and Archives for Edmonton Public Schools. The big, old, brick building and the original 1881 School House are on the same lot at 10425-99 Avenue.

I've worked here since 1984. During this time I have been made aware of the presence of more than one ghost. These phantoms have never tried to frighten me but on several occasions they have interfered with my work. They've unlocked doors that I've locked, turned on and off the boilers, removed pictures from the wall, and scraped furniture across the floor of the room above me when I knew I was the only one in the building.

Once, I'd swear, they had a party. Another man and I spent the last part of a working day setting up a room in the school for an early morning audio-visual presentation. We pulled all the blinds down and stapled them to the sills, lined up chairs in neat rows, and locked the building on our way out.

We were the last to leave that day and the first to arrive the next morning. You can imagine our surprise when we discovered the blinds were up, some right off the windows and lying on the floor. The chairs were knocked over and strewn around the room. We had to really rush in order to redo the room in time for the meeting.

Former staff and students frequently visit the building and many of them have spoken of hauntings and ghosts. With all these strange goings-on I decided to bring an Ouija board.

One ghost, Peter, was quick to identify himself and he maintains that there are half a dozen other spirits floating around. Peter's a very personable character and has "told" me quite a bit about himself. He won't reveal his last name but he has explained that he was a labourer during the construction of the 1912 addition. He was killed in a fall from the roof. It was winter and the ground was frozen. The only place he could be buried was under the floor of the school. Apparently his spirit has roamed the building ever since.

Lately things have been quieter at work. The odd drawer that was shut will be wide open. Pictures may be off the wall or tilted, but I actually wonder if Peter's presence is still as strong as it was.

I asked two young psychics who operate "Second Sight" to come through the school. They confirmed there are a number of ghosts in the building, and the woman was continually drawn to the southwest corner of the addition. Could this possibly be where Peter fell from? I'll probably never know, but that corner does overlook the 1881 School House.

The building was used as a storage shed during the construction of the addition, and so Peter would have been in and out of there frequently. Sometimes when I go out there, a cold shiver passes through me.

It originally opened on Jan. 3, 1882. Peter claims to have died on Jan. 3, 1912. I was born Jan. 3, 1951. Quite a coincidence, isn't it?

42. I Was Awakened by This Same Woman

Velma Grace

The following letter was written in response to one of my requests for "ghost stories." The response was sent to me by Mrs. Velma Grace who is a resident of Keswick, Ont. It describes a house of visions. It would be interesting to know if the current occupants of this house of visions have any strange visions or experiences to report.

July 7, 1990

DEAR SIR:

In answer to your letter requesting information on ghosts, I'm not much of a writer but will do my best and you can take it from there.

My husband and I moved into the back half of a 10-room house. My son and daughter-in-law had the front half, on Leslie Street just north of the Newmarket boundary. This 2-storey house was over 100 years old, with 2-inch thick and 2-foot wide lumber going from the main floor to the roof where the uprights were 4-by-4's with 4-by-4 supports put in from the left bottom corner to the right top corner. It had been a farmhouse. There is still a farm behind it. The house is set well back in off the road. We renovated the place and lived there.

My first experience was awakening to see a halo-like light around an elderly woman with long, gray hair almost to her waist standing in a doorway. I rose up and she disappeared.

I cannot remember how long it was until I was awakened again. This time there was the light and a man, a woman, and a child of about 10, also in the same doorway. They were there and they disappeared when I rose up, the same as my first encounter.

We lived there for 2 years, and 5 times after that I was awakened by this same woman standing beside my bed putting a shroud over me. I raised my arms, and each time I pushed the shroud away, she would disappear. This upset me so that I would wake up screaming, and my husband would come to me and try to console me. I used a Bible plus I wore a necklace with a cross. I also spoke to a woman who offered to come and exorcise the house.

My daughter-in-law would hear music playing when there was no one home but herself. She would also find things moved from where she had put them. On advice from Dr. Dennison of Newmarket, we sold the house as it was too much of a strain on me.

This went on from about 1982 to 1984. The house is at 17740 Leslie Street. I don't know whether this will help you or not.

Yours truly,
Velma Grace

P.S. I was 62 and it made me a nervous wreck.

43. Most People Would Write Off My "Haunting"

Barbara Neyedly

Barbara Neyedly is the publisher of Toronto's Mid-town Voice, a monthly community paper published for downtown Toronto.

She is an able and intuitive person who enjoys meeting people and sharing experiences. On 2 Aug. 1990, she responded to my request for "extraordinary experiences" by sending me two unusual experiences of her own. It is obvious that while castles, crypts, and cathedrals may be the proper dwelling place for ghosts and apparitions, poltergeists and spirits, they are also encountered in modern highrise apartment buildings and townhouse complexes.

Here are her experiences. Make of them what you will.

1.

AROUND 1970, I was living in a three-bedroom apartment in the Thorncliffe Park area of Toronto with my three children, aged ten, eleven, and thirteen.

I had taken up with a handsome Jamaican ten years my junior, and he was often at my apartment. Although from dissimilar backgrounds, at the time we shared a strong emotional bond. This emotional bond, I later came to believe, was at least partly responsible for the dramatic incidence of telepathy that took place one evening.

That night, after the children had gone to bed, my friend and I decided to have a drink of wine and then go outside for a walk around the neighbourhood. It was in late May, about eight-thirty, and it was still light outside. I went into my bedroom, at the end of a long corridor, intending to make up the bed with freshly laundered sheets before having a drink.

I remember that I was fitting the corner of the bottom sheet to the mattress corner closest to the window when it happened. My head snapped up. I saw my boyfriend leering through the outside window pane, just a few inches away — arms reaching toward me, hands curled into claws. He was in the classic "pouncing" position. His eyes were dilated, and his mouth formed a mock-menacing grin.

My screams of shock woke my daughters in the next room. They came running to see what was wrong. The figure was still at the window as I left the bedroom and hurtled myself down the long corridor.

Only later did I remember that there was no balcony outside the third-floor room, just a rough roof, hard, almost impossible to reach from our apartment balcony. The representation of my boyfriend was completely persuasive, down to the detail of the white knit shirt he was wearing that day.

When I reached the living-room a few seconds later, the reality of the apparition leaped out from behind the sofa to scare me "for real." It was a carbon-copy lunge of what I had just seen at the window! I began berating my boyfriend for frightening me through the window. It took him several moments to convince me that he had not actually been out on the roof. He laughingly protested that he had not scared me through the window.

I eventually realized it was an impossibility for him to be able to run across the roof, leap over the railing, travel across the balcony, go through the sliding glass doors, race across the room, and be there behind the sofa to scare me in the few seconds it took me to cover the hall.

But I definitely saw him there, and we spent most of the rest of the evening discussing how such a thing could possibly have happened. The only real clue I ever found was what my boyfriend told me he was thinking about around that time.

When I went to make the bed, he went into the kitchen to take the wine bottle out of the fridge. And on opening the fridge door, he had a strong thought that he should scare me. It would be a joke. He would frighten me when I returned to the living-room.

That is when I think I must have suddenly seen his image at the window, doing what he thought about doing. His thought somehow communicated itself to my unconscious mind, which produced a powerful image of what he suggested, right before my startled eyes.

I don't know how it actually happened. But I believe people who are attuned emotionally, somehow, when the time is right, create the right "climate" for telepathic thought. People who have never experienced anything similar, and who also deny the existence of phenomena outside the five senses, usually tell me that I was dreaming or drunk.

No way.

2.

I couldn't say whether the night's events had anything to do with the street number of the condominium, 1666 Queen Street East, but later I wondered about that. I did find out — much later, as well — that another resident of the townhouse complex, who lived a couple of doors away, also saw a ghost while living there.

I lived at Townhouse Number 12 from 1976, the year the condos were built, until 1986. The houses were on the tall, Elizabethan model, with multiple floors and several small flights of stairs.

It was a blustery, winter night, a Saturday, in 1985 when, highly unusual for me, I fell asleep on the couch about 1:00 a.m. The couch was in the living-room, which was located on the very bottom floor, facing the front entrance.

I don't now remember the reason I didn't make it up the three flights of stairs to my bedroom before conking out. I only recall being overwhelmed by a delicious, drowsy sensation, so overpowering that I fell asleep, leaving several lights on. I had had a few glasses of wine with dinner, hours earlier, but I was not inebriated. In any case, booze has never, before or since, caused me to believe I saw what was not there.

I was not alone in the house. A visitor, who unlike me had made it to bed, was presumably sleeping peacefully four flights above my head.

I awoke suddenly to find all in darkness. I was surprised, as well, to find myself still on the couch. After a few moments my attention was drawn to the carpeted staircase which led one flight up to the kitchen. A young man appeared and began to descend the stairs a few feet away from where I was reclining, bemusedly watching. I noted a tall figure, serious demeanour, longish coat, slightly long hair. Seeing by his face that he was in his twenties, I concluded that he had been visiting my twenty-year-old tenant, Hayley, whose room was located two flights up. But I had forgotten that she was out for the evening and it was unlikely that she had given the key to anyone.

My faint greeting of "hello" was neither noted nor returned, and later I recalled that this unexpected "visitor" never once looked at me or appeared to see me. Rather, he kept looking to the right, over my head, seemingly at a distant scene, as he walked steadily past me towards the door.

Even stranger, I assumed that he would put on boots at the front door, before going out into the elements. But afterwards, try as I might, I couldn't recall that he did, or that he opened the door, walking out, or shut the door behind himself either.

Instead, simultaneously with this person's disappearance in the direction of the front door, I fell back into a deep sleep on the couch. I was reawakened only by the return of my tenant, Hayley, at 4:00 a.m. Of course, she denied having had a visitor in the house that night during her absence, and it now became obvious to my once-drowsy, now sharply awakened senses that the idea was truly far-fetched, even nonsensical. It had only been a spur-of-the-moment rationalization for coping with the fact of the young man's presence in the house.

At this point, you may be tempted to conclude that I had experienced a very vivid dream while deeply asleep. But the proof that it had been real came from Hayley's news that an electrical power failure had plunged our part of the city into darkness a few hours earlier.

This explained, of course, how I had gone to sleep with blazing lights and how I had wakened up to complete darkness, after which I saw our visitor.

My next thought was that it had been a break-in. We had had three break-ins, such occurrences being more frequent than the appearances of ghosts in the neighbourhood. But when Hayley and I checked the only possible point of entry — the sliding glass back door — we confronted an unbroken surface of sparkling, pristine snow. Not even one footprint! It was only at that moment that I realized something without an ordinary explanation had happened!

Again, most people would write off my "haunting" as some form of vivid dream state. It's true that many of the details have escaped my memory. But I was definitely awake and I definitely saw the figure, though I was in an unusually relaxed, even languorous, state of mind at the time. I believe it was that very deep relaxation that made my mind receptive to seeing my ghost, and that it helped to lift the curtain to expose what it is that is usually obscured and what most of us glimpse only rarely or never.

Interestingly, a few years later I had occasion to meet, once again, a couple who had lived only a few townhouses from ours at the same time we lived there. They had also moved away. We got to discussing our old abodes, the people, and the problems. I mentioned, jokingly, that on top of everything else, I had even seen a ghost there.

The wife told me that she had also seen one, but that neither she nor her husband told anyone about it. "They'd think we're crazy," she said. It turned out that one evening she had been seated alone in her dining area, two floors above the ground level, when she was more than startled to see a man, clearly dressed in black, 19th-century clothing. His head was topped by a tall, stovepipe hat. He stood there for a moment and then walked right through the wall!

Before the townhouse complex had been built, there had only been an old service station in that location, about two blocks east of Coxwell Avenue on Queen. Before that, old records show a creek covering the site.

Why it is that relatively new housing units should experience ghosts, a phenomenon normally associated with old houses in which many lives have been lived, is still a puzzle to me. Maybe someday research will reveal the reason.

44. I Immediately Felt Unwanted

Joan Y. Clodd

The words "haunted house" spring to mind.

Indeed, are houses haunted? Or are people haunted? Perhaps the inhabitants of certain houses are haunted. Could it be that their occupants are specially sensitive to the spirit of place or the spirits of the place?

These are some of the questions raised in this letter written by Joan Y. Clodd of Oakville, Ont.

May 26, 1990

DEAR MR. COLOMBO:

I saw your letter in *Oakville Today* and thought you may be interested in my experience.

My father had passed away and I was breaking up his house, preparing to rent it. The house was built in 1925 and had been moved from one side of the creek in Oakville to the other.

Anyway, my cousin, mother-in-law, and I had worked all day of April 10, 1984, packing and cleaning. Later on that evening, we had come back to my new home, when I realized I had left our kettle at my dad's.

It was about 8:00 p.m. I drove up, still with my mother-in-law and my ten-year-old daughter. I opened the door and reached for the light switch. I immediately felt unwanted and very fearful. However, I carried on in. My daughter went in and began looking for her dolls.

The light would not work in the basement where the dolls were. My mother-in-law scurried in, lifted something, and scurried out again. All the while I was feeling, "Get out! Get out!" My daughter began to cry and called out for help. The dolls were lost in darkness. I shone a light for her and she was also fearful. She ran out and I was left alone in the deserted house.

I knew it was not my dad because the energy was very angry and did not want to be disturbed. I was frozen for a few moments. Then I ran out too.

When we pulled away in the car, my mother-in-law asked if I had felt "something." Now, this lady does not "feel things." In fact, she does not give any credibility to anything "spooky." When I told her I had felt "something," we compared notes and found similar fears. I went back the next morning and felt nothing at all.

About six months later I had a reading done by a medium who did not know me or anything about me. She said a woman called Bertha was saying she was sorry for being aggressive with me at my dad's house and did not mean to frighten me. I was pleased and amazed all at once. You see, I never really met a real spirit before although I have been interested for years. In fact, I was sorry I had run away. I should have tried to speak to her.

The tenants of the house never complained so I don't know if Bertha only made herself known to us.

I hope you find this of interest.

Yours truly,
Joan Y. Clodd

P.S. I must tell you I have dealt with spirits for years as I was a practising psychic and I have never run into a negative energy before. I think that was what made me fearful. All the spirits I had dealt with were lost or helpful. I have also cleaned out houses where spirits were trapped and encountered no fear.

I tend to channel without being aware and this becomes difficult for me. I hope you can use my experience for your work. I have read some of your work with interest.

J. Y. C.

45. The Picture Had Hung Quietly

Anthony B. Sant

Anthony B. Sant heard me on Toronto radio station Q-107 one afternoon as I was holding forth on paranormal experiences for Bill Carroll of "Barometer." The listener contacted me later that day, and one week later he sent me the text of the following letter, which arrived on 19 April 1990. (Note the preponderance of the number nine!) The letter speaks for itself.

DEAR MR. COLOMBO:

I am a 34-year-old artist and big fan of rock-'n'-roll music. I also supplement my meagre income by winning radio phone-in contests from Toronto area radio stations. To date I have won between 50 and 60 contests since July '86. I feel compelled to relate an incident which happened in Winona, Ont., in December 1989.

This all began earlier, in 1986, when I created a pen-and-ink portrait of John Lennon that I gave to my 22-year-old sister Tracy as a Christmas present. She framed this 11"-by-14" sketch and later gave it to her boyfriend John Jemison. Soon after, John hung this picture upon the living-room wall of his home in Winona.

On Friday, December 8th, 1989, my sister Tracy was over at her boyfriend John's place with his roommate Steve Moro and their married friends, Pat and Marcel Blais. Tracy and John stepped out to do some grocery shopping, while Steve and the rest stayed at the house watching T.V. and playing dart games. The T.V. was tuned to

Tony Sant

MuchMusic (the music video channel) and the show they were watching was a documentary about the life of John Lennon. It was being shown to commemorate the ninth anniversary of Lennon's murder.

While Pat and Marcel and Steve were playing darts, they could hear and see a re-creation of Lennon's murder on the T.V. About the same time as they heard the shot fired on the T.V., they heard a crash behind them. Looking around, to their utter amazement, they saw that the picture of Lennon had crashed to the floor. Oddly enough, the picture was undamaged. John's dog, Reba, went crazy, yelping and barking as if terrified.

When Tracy and John came back, they found their friends in a state of fearful excitement. Steve said that it was as if somebody had grabbed the picture and thrown it down from the wall. Now this picture had hung quietly for over a year without any problem despite the comings and goings of many people.

There are a few funny things about this incident. One is the name of the place where this occurred. In 1969, John Lennon changed his middle name from Winston to Ono (his wife's surname). If you take the first three letters of "Winston" and add them to "Ono," you get a close approximation to the name of the town — Winona.

The other, more obvious, oddity is that this happened on the ninth anniversary of John Lennon's death-day. If you read any biographies of Lennon, usually mention is made of the fact that the number nine is the most important number in his life. He was born on October 9th just as his son Sean was. He even wrote three songs about the number nine — "Revolution 9," "One after 909," and "No. 9 Dream." In "Revolution 9" a voice repeats "number nine" over and over again. The probability of these incidents occurring together — the T.V. show about John Lennon's murder on the ninth annivesary of his death and the picture falling down at the same time — are quite astronomical. One in several million, I would guess.

I swear that as far as I can tell this story is absolutely true.

Yours truly,
Tony Sant

46. "Is That You, Tara?"

Frank Chatain

The following letter was written by Frank Chatain who lives in Port Hardy, B.C. It was sent to me on 25 June 1990. I am reproducing it pretty well as it was written, with only routine copy editing.

The account makes harrowing reading.

UPON SEEING YOUR AD in the *North Island News*, the compulsion to write to you was very strong.

I am forty-seven years old. In 1986, two weeks before her seventeenth birthday, our daughter was killed in a car accident. This accident occurred in Victoria, where my wife and I lived at the time. Tara had my wife's car, and for some unknown reason, she had apparently let the younger brother of her girlfriend drive the car for a short distance of four city blocks to the store. It would seem that he took a corner too fast or lost control because he drove into a hydro pole with a street-light on top. We were told that she died instantly of a broken neck.

Now I have told the story that follows to three couples, our closest friends. One couple told me right after that they did not believe in that kind of thing. The second couple told me that they do believe in that kind of thing happening. The third couple, with scepticism written on their faces, preferred to remain neutral.

After the tragic accident, many of our old friends came to

Victoria to visit us. Two of my daughter's friends came from Kelowna and they spent a week with us. They had to be at the bus depot before 5:00 a.m. in order to be on the first bus out. Naturally I drove them there and left them as they embarked on the 5:00 a.m. bus. There is very little traffic so early in the morning. I drove over to the sea wall, and then I drove around the city until I found myself parked kitty-corner from the pole where my daughter had been killed.

I looked up. The street-light on the pole was still on, but it was dimmer than the rest of the street-lights. That fatal night I had made the police sergeant, who drove my wife and me to identify our daughter, stop the car so we could see the scene of the accident. That night the light on the pole was off.

So as I sat there, looking up at it, I wondered in my mind if Tara might still be here. Just then the light blinked off and on. I said in my mind, "I suppose the light has a short in it because of the impact." The light went off for a brief moment, then came back on. In my mind I said, "Is that you, Tara?" The light went very, very bright and I thought it was burning itself out. But it returned to its dim state. I then thought, "Are you trying to tell me something, Tara?" The light flickered bright and back to dim a few times. I thought to myself, "Oh, sure, whatever I knew about Morse Code I've forgotten." So I said, "Can you give me a light out for a 'no' and a brighter for a 'yes'?" The light went brighter. I thought, "What do you want me to do, Tara? Should I go break that s.o.b.'s neck?" I was thinking about the driver of the car. The light went out for a brief instant and came back on dim. I then said, in my mind, "Do you want me to do nothing and leave him alone?" The light went very bright and then dim again. I then said, "Are you all right where you are?" The light went very bright. I said, "Should I come back tomorrow night?" The light went off. I said, "Do you want me to go home to Mom?" and the light went very bright. I said, "Okay, goodbye, my girl," and the light flickered and then it stayed on with the same brightness as the rest of the street-lights. I drove home.

As I did handyman work in the huge apartment complex where we lived, I had no need of a car. My wife's car had been totalled, so we found ourselves in need of some form of transportation. We went to the second-hand car lot nearest our home. My wife and I, still living in a stunned state, were walking around like zombies with a salesman pointing out the best buys. I found myself looking over a Chrysler, a car I have always admired. My wife and the salesman had wandered away from me, as this car was not in the price range I had specified. After I rejoined them, my wife and I decided to go home and come back the next morning, and perhaps test drive a few cars.

Upon our return in the morning, we found the salesman waiting for us beside four cars that he had lined up in the driveway. The Chrysler was the third car in line. The first car we drove was a small one and we were considering buying it when I decided to try the defrost. Instantly I received a mouthful of old dust. Without thinking, my wife and I both said together, "Tara doesn't want us to have this car."

On our return to the car lot, I went directly to the Chrsyler with its clean, white seats and sat in it. As I got behind the wheel I felt as if someone or something had touched my heart. I can't explain it. One moment I didn't care if I lived or died, and the next moment I was feeling full of joy. I called to my wife and the salesman who was changing the plates to the second car in line. I said I wanted to try the Chrysler next and we did. Although my wife did not feel a touch to her heart, she fell in love with the car, and we bought it on our return to the car lot. Now we had a big car and we thought we'd get out of Victoria where so many memories lay. We decided to come to Port Hardy to visit our friends who had moved out there. It is three hundred miles from Victoria and we were persuaded by our friends to get a change of scenery.

It was already late in the day before we got going; therefore we ended up driving by night, which comes early during the winter months. Winter on the island is not always snow. It's mostly rain and we got our share that night. As there is nothing between Campbell River and Port Hardy, a driver tends to put the pedal down a bit more than necessary. As we enjoyed the loud music on the tape deck, each of us lost in our own thoughts, the headlights suddenly went off. Now, this is a road in the middle of the forest in the middle of the night. As I applied the brakes gently, so as not to cause us to spin, the lights started to blink on and off. I stopped the car and we sat in the darkness for a moment before going out in the pouring rain to look at the headlights as if we could do something about them. Not seeing anything broken on the front, I walked to the back of the car. The lights had come back on, and as my wife was getting back into the car, she said, "Is that you, Tara?" and the lights blinked on and off. I had seen this last flash and my wife told me what she had said. My wife suggested that I drive slower, which I did, and within two miles we encountered a really sharp curve which we never would have made at the speed I was going on the wet blacktop. Needless to say, we attribute this to our daughter's intervention.

Upon seeing our friends, we recounted the story of the lights, to which my friend said, "Oh, yeah! I had a Chrysler and they all do that." He figured that I probably needed a new alternator, which we had checked and replaced. Since then, four years ago, we have enjoyed our car. I have found bare wires and taped them up. I have removed the back window stoplight, which did not come with the car. I have disconnected the tape deck which had a short in it. In short, I have been over the car with a fine-tooth comb and still we'll be going along at night and the lights will blink and sure enough around the next curve there will be a deer standing on the road. My wife and I have had many such nights. Our son, who is in the Air Force and stationed in a different province, came home by plane. When I drove to the airport to pick him up, the headlights blinked on and off almost all the way there. We had told our son about the happenings. When he was in the car and we were driving out of the airport towards the highway, the lights began to blink off and on again. My wife said to our boy, "Say hello to Tara," at which my boy got a big unbelieving smile on his face. I said, "Better say hello to her or the lights will blink like that all the way home." He said, "Hello, Tara," and the lights stayed on all the way home. A few nights later my wife and my son were going along the island highway. My son was driving, when all of a sudden the lights started to blink off and on and he said to his mother, "I better get this fixed for Dad before I go back," and my wife said, "Just slow down, there's probably something on the road." Sure enough, there was a huge dog right in his lane. As soon as he slowed down the lights stayed normal and quit blinking. It made a believer out of our son the night he took the car by himself and went speeding along until the lights started to blink. Then he slowed down in time to avoid a radar trap the police had set up.

My wife and I are not stupid and we don't see ghosts all over the place. We are both working, normal people. We have accepted our loss and we are living with it.

There are many other coincidences in our lives, too many to mention.

47. A Very Strange Experience

Margaret Fyfe

*From time to time, some people report, the experi-
ence of the reality of the world seems to wax and wane. It recedes
from their senses and memories. It does not always return. Familiar
things take on a curiously unfamiliar aspect; unfamiliar things
assume a surprisingly familiar form. Such experiences are quite
striking and unsettling and make a strong impression on memory.
Psychiatrists, observing elements of dissociation, speak of the condition they called* derealization. *Psychologists, noting the ability of
memory to knit the factual and the fictitious into a seamless whole,
refer to* confabulation. *Parapsychologists are free to talk about
altered states of consciousness and other dimensions of reality.*

*Here is one account of the familiar becoming unfamiliar — or the
unfamiliar becoming familiar. Margaret Fyfe is not the author's real
name. It is a pseudonym adopted for the purpose of publishing this
reminiscence by a well-known Canadian writer. The reminiscence
was written in October 1989 and it refers to her experience in
England in August of the previous year.*

LAST SUMMER I had a very strange experience. I was going to a
festival in England, and needed to reserve a room before I left
Canada. The festival was being held in the seaside town of Sidmouth which is quite small and very popular so hotels tend to fill
up early.

I phoned the festival office and asked them to see if they could find a room for me, saying I would phone again the next day. When I called the second time I was told that the Devoran Hotel had a cancellation and that I should phone Mrs. Clifford at Sidmouth 3151. I said that was fine because I'd stayed at the Devoran the year before and had liked it. Accordingly I phoned the number and booked for the week. When I mentioned that I had stayed there for a few days the previous summer, Mrs. Clifford said I hadn't, because she booked only by the week.

When I got to London I took a train from Paddington to Honiton, the railway station closest to Sidmouth, and got a taxi there, telling the driver to take me to the Devoran Hotel. When we reached Sidmouth I remembered the hotel's location and directed the driver to it. When we got there, it looked just as I remembered it. However, when I went in I didn't recognize Mrs. Clifford. Thinking that the hotel might have changed hands, I asked how long she had been there and she told me fifteen years. I then noticed some differences to what I remembered. The desk was placed at right angles to the front door while I remembered it as being parallel last year. The dining-room was on the opposite side of the front hall to what I remembered. However, the location was just as I remembered, and when I started going to the various festival programs I knew exactly how to reach them from the Devoran. The whole block was familiar to me, and there was no other hotel in it that looked enough like the Devoran for me to think that that was where I had stayed.

Another strange point was that the previous year the festival office had given me a phone number to book a room, saying it was for the Elizabeth Hotel. I had called and made my booking, but when, on reaching the town, I went to the Elizabeth Hotel, which was at the corner of a block, they had no record of my booking. I showed the clerk the phone number I had been given and he said it might be for the Devoran, which was right next door. I went into the Devoran, and they had my reservation. The confusion over the phone number and hotel name apparently resulted from the fact that the Devoran and the Elizabeth were together on the festival office's alphabetical listing. If my memory was wrong on this point, it might have been the Elizabeth Hotel I stayed at the previous year.

However, it was considerably larger than the Devoran: I remembered it, but it didn't seem to me that I had stayed there.

This confusion naturally puzzzled me, and during the week I was there I tried to think of some explanation. I looked at all the hotels in the block where I knew I had stayed, and none except the Devoran looked familiar. When I came home I looked to see if I had kept my receipt from the previous year, but I hadn't. Thus, this experience remains a mystery to me.

48. The Sticky Man

Donna Schillaci

In a local newspaper, Donna Schillaci, a mother who lives in Oakville, Ont., saw my letter inviting readers to send me their true-life "ghost stories."

Ms. Schillaci had a scary experience to relate, one that involved not only herself but also her young son Adam. She sent me one account of "the sticky man" on 5 June 1990 and then, on 22 June 1990, a second, fuller account. It is the second account that is being reproduced here.

One cannot help but wonder: Is there a "sticky man" in the basement of her house? Is the spirit there still, biding time until the appropriate moment when it will reappear?

June 22, 1990

DEAR MR. COLOMBO:

As I'm writing this letter to you I can't help but wonder if anyone could possibly understand or even believe what both my small son Adam and I experienced. But I guess that's what you want to hear about.

About a year and a half ago, when Adam was almost two years old, we moved into an older house. I think the house was between eighty and ninety years old. I never felt anything unusual about the house when we first moved in, but as time went on I felt a heaviness about the walls. I ignored the feeling.

161

Then one day, while in the basement, I felt the heaviness again. It was stronger this time. I noticed the furnace room door was more open than usual. Perhaps in vacuuming I had bumped into it. I couldn't remember.

And then I saw it — its form transparent so I could see the bricks of the wall through it. What caught my eye most of all was the figure's face. It was male. His eyes were leering and devilishly playful. He seemed to be challenging me — and in a frightening way.

I ran back upstairs as fast as I could. I tried to pretend I had imagined it all. It was hard. The bathroom, the shower, the tub were all down there in the basement, and when I went down there I had to feel comfortable.

Thereafter, as much as possible, I tried to keep the furnace room door closed. Some days I felt something in there, other days nothing. Gradually I began to forget about it all.

Then one day, while I was showering in the basement, Adam screamed from outside the shower curtains. It was a horrible scream, one I had never heard from him before. I shakingly opened the curtain and asked him what was wrong. He screamed, "Mommie, a sticky man on the wall!"

I quickly climbed out of the tub, looked around, and tried as best I could to see something where he pointed with his tiny finger. There was nothing there. He kept saying, "Sticky man, sticky man!" Instead of asking Adam too many questions, I knelt beside him and told him it was all pretend. He calmed down.

The first time this happened my explanation was enough. Yet it happened two more times. And always it was a "sticky man" he saw. Early one evening Adam was dancing in the kitchen. He got strangely delirious with joy and laughter. With both arms waving to the music he loudly cried out, "Sticky man is coming upstairs!"

Frightened, I yelled out powerfully for the "sticky man" to go back downstairs and to leave us alone. I ranted, raged, and repeatedly stamped my feet at the edge of the basement steps. I stated it wasn't fair. He was frightening a little child. I never let on he was scaring the skin off my face, too.

From that evening on, we were no longer bothered by his appearances. And if I did "feel" him around, I bravely and confidently spoke out. My commands were simple. Go away. Sometimes my tone would soften and I would pray for this poor soul to find its way back to God because I instinctively sensed he was lost. But I always made it very clear — I didn't want him around.

I try not to talk to Adam about his experiences. I have to admit I'd love to know how much he does remember. Six months ago he asked if mommy remembered the "sticky man." A jolt of panic sped up my spine. I looked sadly into his clear hazel eyes, quickly nodded yes, and changed the subject. I don't want him to be afraid of life, and I don't want him believing in ghosts. I'm firm about that. Yet it's too late. He's constantly zapping ghosts with an imaginary gun. Maybe he's lucky: he hasn't associated "sticky man" with ghosts. I really don't know.

As for myself, I still feel my stomach turn whenever I talk about it. No matter how much courage I mustered up in facing it, there was always fear not far behind. But I have to admit I'm stronger for having stood up to a...can I say it?...a ghost!

Sincerely,
Donna Schillaci

49. A Large White Persian Cat

Brenda P. Baltensperger

"*I read, with interest, your letter in the local newspaper for stories of parapsychological happenings and think you might be interested in what I have to say.*"

So wrote Brenda P. Baltensperger, a resident of Goderich, Ont., in her letter to me, dated 12 June 1990. She was responding to my open letter carried by the London Free Press.

I am reproducing Mrs. Baltensperger's letter because it is uncommonly interesting. How does one account for such events or experiences?

Mrs. Baltensperger ended her letter in this fashion: "I hope this is the sort of thing you're looking for. If you'd like to visit us any time, you're welcome. I can't promise any results, though, as they are unpredictable."

The next time I am in the vicinity of Goderich, I plan to pay a visit to the Baltensperger residence — but not if it's a stormy night!

IN THE FALL OF 1989, Peter and I moved into a turn-of-the-century house in Goderich. We have two cats that seemed quite content with their new home. They would accompany me to bed where I would read for an hour before going to sleep.

One evening, while Peter was away in Toronto for a few days, I went to bed around ten o'clock, as usual, to read. About ten-thirty, a storm erupted, mildly at first, and then grew in strength. I heard a low growl from Max, the cat sitting beside me. When I looked up, his hair was standing up along his back. He was wild-eyed. I assumed it was the storm and looked over to the foot of the bed where Jenny, the other cat, had been curled up asleep. She was staring wide-eyed and had crouched back as far as she could in the corner of the bed.

Suddenly I was aware of a large, white Persian cat padding across the bed towards me, its tail straight up in welcome. My first reaction was, "How the hell did that get into the house?" I knew that I had locked both doors and there was no access through the windows. About arm's-length distance, the cat disappeared. It looked as solid as one of my own cats. The storm dissipated, but the cats remained agitated, so I let them sleep with me for the night.

A few months later, early spring, I was watching television. Max was curled up asleep on the chesterfield across from me and Jenny, likewise, beside me. The wind picked up and howled around the house. Suddenly Max stood up, hair bristling, and stared towards the open door of the sitting-room. Jenny whimpered and nestled as close and low as she could to me.

Through the open door I could see, on the small landing at the top of the stairs, the white Persian cat. It trotted down the stairs, and as it stepped into the hallway, about four feet from where I was sitting, it disappeared.

This appearance has been repeated twice since then, the last time about two weeks ago when we had a really vicious storm. Unfortunately, Peter has yet to see the white Persian cat.

I have done a little research on parapsychology. (Peter and I were planning to write a book on the subject when we lived in St. Catharines.) I am convinced that the effect is a magnetic impression due to the possible magnetic lines running through our property.

I have inquired in the neighbourhood if any previous owners of the house had a white Persian cat, but no one remembers anything. If it had only been my own impression, I would have said I was hallucinating, but the cats certainly did react to something.

The couple who live in an 1897 house across the road from us also have a "ghost." They, and visitors to the house, have heard someone walking about the upstairs hallway at night. Also, Verne, who has been quite ill, has awakened at night to find a tall, severe woman in a dark-coloured Victorian dress standing over her bed. A friend of hers, who is some sort of psychic, can't bear to be in the house. She says she senses a presence that is ominous and overbearing. I told them to write to you also, but I don't know whether they will or not.

50. Mackenzie King's Ghost

Percy J. Philip

"Mackenzie King's Ghost" is the title I have given to the following series of articles, columns, talks, etc.

They circle around the subject of whether or not in 1954 the late and former Prime Minister William Lyon Mackenzie King (1875-1950) made a ghostly appearance for the purpose of communicating with his valued confidant, Percy J. Philip. The question remains, as they say, open....

During his lifetime it was a closely guarded secret, shared only with intimate friends and associates, that Mackenzie King was a closet spiritualist. No one knows whether or not the late Prime Minister believed in the tenets of spiritualism. What is known for certain is that he practised the methods of spiritualism. He consulted mediums, he practised table-rapping, and he believed in omens. Following his death, the closely guarded secret of his spiritualistic interests became common knowledge.

Here is the strange but true story of how one man was affected by the legacy...the spirit, if you wish...of William Lyon Mackenzie King. Appended to it is some material of related interest. In chronological order, with all its errors and confusions, is how the story unfolds....

1. Mysterious Conversation

A SCOTSMAN BY BIRTH and a newspaper man by profession, Percy J. Philip had many strange experiences in the course of his 24 years as a *New York Times* correspondent in Paris and Ottawa. Once, during the panic period of the war, in May, 1940, a mob of excited Parisians mistook him for a German parachutist. An improvised execution squad of runaway soldiers and peasants with shot-guns was all ready to shoot him when two gendarmes arrived and, in the name of republican law and order, prevented that error from being committed. But nothing, Philip says, was as strange as the story he will tell on CBC Trans-Canada, September 24th at 7:45 p.m. of a conversation he had last summer with the late W. L. Mackenzie King. Philip is not a spiritualist, he says; he is just a newspaper reporter, now retired, and has done his best to make this an objective report!

Source: "Mysterious Conversation," *CBC Times*, September 19-25, 1954.

2. Speaker's Choice

Friday, September 24: Trans-Canada Network, Canadian Broadcasting Corporation

7:45 — *Speaker's Choice* Percy Philip, on a conversation with W. L. Mackenzie King.

Source: *CBC Times*, September 19-25, 1954

3. Speaker's Choice: Announcer's Introduction

Our speaker tonight is Mr. Percy Philip, a Scotsman by birth, a newspaper man by profession and, as correspondent for the *New York Times* in Paris, and later in Ottawa, he had many strange experiences....

Source: Program Notes for *Speaker's Choice*, September 24, 1954.

4. Spirit of Mackenzie King in Garden — *"WRITER SITS ON PARK BENCH SAYS HE TALKED WITH MACKENZIE KING SPIRIT"* By Ben Rose, Star Staff Correspondent

Ottawa, Sept. 25 — Percy Philip, former *New York Times* correspondent and for many years a friend of the late W. L.

Mackenzie King, said last night that in June of this year he had a conversation with the former prime minister, who has been dead for four years.

In a CBC radio talk, Mr. Philip, now 68, who represented the *New York Times* in Ottawa for 12 years, said the conversation took place on a park bench at nearby Kingsmere, Que., where Mr. King had his summer home.

Mr. Philip said he was sitting alone on the park bench when suddenly he became aware of a "presence" beside him.

"There were no sighs, groans or lightning flashes such as mark a spirit's arrival on the Shakespearian stage," he said. "There was, if anything, a deep peace." He said he did not turn his head but said as naturally as he could: "Good evening, Mr. King."

"Good evening, Philip. I am so glad you spoke to me," Mr. Philip quoted him as replying.

The conversation, Mr. Philip said, ranged from politics to international affairs. "But there was no pessimism, no warning of catastrophe in the comment on human affairs," he said.

During his lifetime the late Mr. King was a believer in spiritualism. Mr. Philip says he is not a spiritualist but he liked Mr. King "and he liked me. We often took walks together, with his dog, Pat, and he often invited me to dinner at Laurier House."

The newspaperman said that at one point Mr. King, who held office longer than any other prime minister in the Commonwealth, mused: "It is a disadvantage to a democracy when any party remains either in or out of office too long. It loses touch with the deep instincts of the people."

At another point Mr. Philip quoted Mr. King as complaining that none of his old colleagues ever come to Kingsmere to visit him.

"I am still near enough to my earthly life to want to hear the gossip and to chat as we have done. But no one has ever come," Mr. King is reported to have said. "Probably they are so busy with their careers that they have forgotten me — and yet I have helped a good many of them along the road."

The conversation lasted two hours, said Mr. Philip. As to doubts that he really had the conversation, he said: "I don't just think I did it. I am convinced that I did it and, I repeat, it seemed an entirely normal and natural thing to do, although I know perfectly well the

the former prime minister had been dead for four years.

"On that June evening there were no other visitors. The air was clear and cool. I sat down on a bench beside the ruins and began thinking about the strange little man who loved his hill-top home so dearly. I suppose I was in what is called a receptive condition. I know I was conscious that I was not alone. There was someone on that park bench beside me."

In a warm tone, which always marked his conversations, the voice of Mr. King spoke to him, Mr. Philip said.

"I was thinking of you," Mr. Philip said he told the late prime minister.

"Oh, yes," Mr. King replied. "I knew that. But one of the rules which governs our conduct is that we are like the children who must not speak until they are spoken to. I suppose it is a good rule because it would be very disturbing if we went around talking to people. The sad thing is that so few of them ever speak to us."

Mr. Philip said he called his talk "fantasia," because it sounded like that and he realized many persons will not believe it happened.

"I am not sure I believe it myself. But it seemed so real at the time and not in the least unusual. It was indeed so real that it has haunted me ever since, and like the ancient mariner, I have got to tell my tale.

"Of one thing I am sure. Mr. King himself would believe me. He used to have conversations like that with people who had left this world. He talked with his father and mother regularly, with President Lincoln, William Ewart Gladstone and a great many other notables of the past, mostly Liberals."

Mr. Philip said Mackenzie King's official biographer, MacGregor Dawson, has expressed keen interest in his experience at Kingsmere and has asked him to supply full details of his talk with the late prime minister.

"I suppose," Mr. Philip said, "that we are just a little bit scared about beginning a conversation with the unknown. You know how hard it is to speak into a dark, empty room, asking, 'Is there anyone here?' "

"That is certainly a difficulty for many people," said Mr. King. "But the room is never empty. It is often filled with lonely ones who would like to be spoken to. They must, however, be called by name, confidently, affectionately, not challenged to declare themselves."

"Your name," Mr. Philip said, "must often be so mentioned in this lovely place you left to the Canadian people."

"Oh, yes, mentioned," he said Mr. King answered, "but between being mentioned and being addressed by name is a great difference. I have heard things about my character, motives, political action and even my personal appearance and habits which have made me laugh so loudly I thought I must break through the sound barrier. And I have heard things about myself that made me shrink."

Mr. Philip said that in 1945 Mr. King told the Earl of Athlone, then governor general, that he had been speaking to President Roosevelt who died earier that year.

Mr. King was reported to have added during that occasion that life after death should be regarded as a "continuation of the one we know with the same processes of growth and change, until, eventually, we forget our experience on this earth."

Mr. Philip said he had the sensation of being suspended in time and space as Mr. King's quiet voice went on: "There are things that I said and did that I could regret, but on this side we soon learn to have no regrets. Life would be meaningless if we did not all make mistakes and eternity intolerable if we spent it regretting them."

Mr. Philip said the late prime minister seemed to want to hear the latest news, rather than tell him anything. Canadian development during these recent years was what interested him most, the expansion of housing, Kitimat, Ungava, the St. Lawrence seaway and power project, "although I noticed he was not up to date on everything."

"My successor has been lucky," he quoted Mr. King as saying. Mr. Philip added that was as far as he went in any personal reference.

"Canada has been very prosperous. I hope it will continue to be so, but you cannot expect good times always. It is adversity that proves the real value of men and nations," he quoted Mr. King as saying.

Mr. King had praise for the British. "They have shown great political vitality and have come through a revolution both within their own country and in their relations with other peoples, which still lies ahead in America.

"You will remember that I was always opposed to any attempt to institutionalize the Commonwealth and I think I am being proved right. It is still the best bulwark against communism or any other imperialism. Big unions of peoples, such as the Germans, the Russians, even the French, built up under central governments, are apt to grow rank, to become too rigid and dangerous. Harmony among independent peoples in a free association is much safer even if that harmony is not always perfect.

"I think you told me once you are Scottish born and a wee bit fey," Mr. King said. "It's a good thing to be. We have two worlds. Those people who think their world is the only one, and who take it and themselves so seriously, have a very dull time. Do come back and talk with me again."

"I muttered words of thanks for his welcome and the conversation we had had and praised his generosity in bequeathing his estate to the Canadian people," Mr. Philip said.

"Oh, that was half for the people and half for myself," Mr. King replied. "I could never have been happy if the property and home I had acquired, a piece at a time, so lovingly, had been broken up into building lots for a few summer cottagers. I prefer that it should go to the whole people, to all who care to come. Also, I should have had no familiar place to spend my time until I get accustomed to the infinite and eternity."

Mr. Philip concluded: "The smile had become almost impish. Here was the old unrepentant Billy King, one half a great gesture of principle and philanthropy, and the other half a shrewd, wee Aberdonian, looking out for his comfort, even in the afterlife.

" 'Come back again,' " he quoted Mr. King as saying, "as warmly as a ghost can do. But we did not shake hands. That, I thought, would be going too far."

Mr. Philip said his talk with Mr. King took place in June of this year on "one of those good days." The veteran correspondent, who was with the *New York Times* for 33 years, is now living at his summer home at Aylmer, Que., and devotes his time to free-lance writing. He wrote a book which has not yet been published. Mr.

Philip is a colorful figure around Ottawa, a tall scholarly man who always wears a beret and a scarf.

While Mr. King was far more than 25 years a practising spiritualist, he was not a member of the Spiritualist Church but remained a Presbyterian until his death. His beliefs were kept secret for fear scoffers would charge he was conducting the affairs of the nation on advice from the spirit world. And this was not true, according to Mrs. Helen Hughes, a Glasgow medium who sat with him for many years.

In a recent interview she was reported as saying he did not want advice on public affairs but merely to talk with the departed. His communion with the dead was a great comfort to him, she said.

It was said Mr. King became interested in spiritualism because he was a lonely man. What he wanted more than anything from a medium was intimate conversation with his own family. He remained devoted to his mother, his brother, Dr. Macdougall King, and his sister, Isabel, all of whom died within a few years.

Source: Ben Rose, "Spirit of Mackenzie King in Garden — Writer," The *Toronto Star*, 25 Sept. 1954.

5. Radio and Television By Gordon Sinclair

One of the creepiest outputs from CBC's talks department that I've heard in a long time came Friday night, while driving to Muskoka, where I heard Percy Philip, late Ottawa chieftain, of the *New York Times* tell of his meeting in June last, with the late Prime Minister W.L.M. King.

At that time Mr. King had been in his grave more than a year.

But Spiritualist Philip, a man of wide reputation, told of talking with him, on a bench, at Kingsmere which was Mr. King's summer retreat.

The interview was carried fully in Saturday's *Star* but it was a tingling spooky thing as I heard it, because Philip made the impossible seem commonplace.

Everyone in my car...including this sceptic...was satisfied that Philip and Mr. King had, in truth, held their long informative chat.

The dead can't speak. So the puzzle was deep.

Source: Gordon Sinclair, "Radio and Television," The *Toronto Star*, Monday, September 27, 1954.

6. Ghostly Gossip on a Bench with Mackenzie King

Ottawa, Sept. 24 (CP). — Percy Philip, internationally known newspaperman, says he spoke to former Prime Minister Mackenzie King four years after the Liberal leader died. Mr. King was a great believer in spiritualism.

The 68-year-old retired correspondent of the *New York Times* said in a radio talk tonight that his conversation with Mr. King took place three months ago. Mr. King died in July, 1950.

The conversation, he said, took place on a park bench at near-by Kingsmere, Que., where Mr. King had his summer home.

"I sat chatting with Mr. Mackenzie King in the grounds of his old home at Kingsmere for nearly two hours one evening this past summer," said Mr. Philip, who added that he is not a spiritualist.

"I don't just think I did it. I am convinced that I did it and, I repeat, it seemed an entirely normal and natural thing to do, although I knew perfectly well that the former Prime Minister had been dead for four years."

Mr. Philip said he called his talk "fantasic" [sic], because it sounded like that and he realized that many persons will not believe it happened.

"I am not sure that I believe it myself. But it seemed so real at the time and not in the least unusual. It was indeed so real that it has haunted [me] ever since, and like the Ancient Mariner, I have got to tell my tale."

Mr. Philip, who worked for *The New York Times* for 33 years until his retirement in 1953, said he was sitting alone on the park bench when he suddenly became aware of a presence beside him.

"There were no sighs and groans and lightning flashes such as mark a spirit's arrival on the Shakespearian stage. There was, if anything, a deeper peace...."

Mr. Philip said he did not turn his head, but said as naturally as he could: "Good evening, Mr. King."

"Good evening, Philip, I am so glad you spoke to me," Mr. Philip quoted him as replying.

Mr. Philip said the conversation ranged from politics to international affairs, "but there was no pessimism, no warnings of catastrophe in his comment on human affairs."

The newspaperman said that at one point Mr. King, who held office longer than any other Prime Minister in the Commonwealth, mused: "It is a disadvantage to a democracy when any party remains either in or out of office too long. It loses touch with the deep instincts of the people."

At another point Mr. Philip quoted Mr. King as complaining that none of his old colleagues ever came to Kingsmere to visit him.

"I am still near enough to my earthly life to want to hear the gossip and to chat as we have done. But no one has ever come." Mr. King is reported to have said, "Probably they are so busy with their careers that they have forgotten me — and yet I have helped a good many of them along the road."

Mr. Philip said that during Mr. King's lifetime the late Prime Minister claimed to have held conversations with his dead parents, Abraham Lincoln and other notables in history.

He said that in 1945 Mr. King told the Earl of Athlone, then Governor-General, that he had been speaking to President Roosevelt, who died earlier that year.

Mr. King was reported to have added on that occasion that life after death should be regarded as a "continuation of the one we know with the same processes of growth and change, until, eventually, we forget our experience on this earth."

Source: "Ghostly Gossip on a Bench with Mackenzie King," The *Globe and Mail*, Page One, 25 Sept. 1954.

7. I Talked with Mackenzie King's Ghost By Percy J. Philip

On a June evening in 1954 I had a long conversation with the former Canadian Prime Minister William L. Mackenzie King as we sat on a bench in the grounds of his old summer home at Kingsmere, 12 miles from Ottawa. It seemed to me an entirely normal thing although I knew perfectly well that Mr. King had been dead for four years.

Of course, when I returned to Ottawa and told my story nobody quite believed me. I myself became just the least bit uncertain as to whether it really had happened, or at least as to how it had happened. Did I fall asleep and dream? Was this due to paranormal circumstances which cannot be explained?

Of one thing I am sure. Mr. King himself would believe me. He once held similar conversations — almost daily in some cases — with persons who had left this world. He talked with his father and mother regularly and with great men and women of the past. His diary, in which he recorded his spiritual experiences, as well as his political activities and contacts, gives detailed accounts of these conversations. Unfortunately it is not likely to be published in full because his will provided that certain parts should be destroyed. His literary executors feel bound to carry out these instructions.

It was not until after his death that the Canadian people learned that their bachelor, liberal Prime Minister communed with the dead both directly and, occasionally, through mediums. When it did become known — in a rather sensational way — it shocked many.

Yet the Prime Minister made no secret of his beliefs and practices. To friends who had lost dear ones he wrote in this manner: "I know how you feel. It seems as though you cannot bear to go on without that wonderful companionship and affection. But let me assure you that love still exists. A bond as strong as that is not broken by death or anything else. Your father is still near you. If you can be still and listen and feel, you will realize he is close to you all your life. I know that because it is so with my mother and me."

That quotation is from one of the many hundreds of letters of condolence which Mr. King wrote with his own hand for he was punctilious in such matters. At funerals he always spoke similar words of comfort to those bereaved. Otherwise, although he made no secret of his beliefs, he did not parade them.

Once, at Government House, about Christmas time in 1945, he told the Governor General, the Earl of Athlone, that he had spoken with President Roosevelt the previous night. "President Truman, you mean," said the Governor. The Earl saw that some of his staff were making signs from behind Mr. King's back, evidently trying to convey some message. He was puzzled but, being a good constitutional Governor General, he kept quiet and did not again correct the Prime Minister when he repeated, "Oh, no, I mean the late President Roosevelt."

The occasion of the incident was the showing of the Noel Coward film, "Blythe [sic] Spirit," which Mr. King found "most interesting."

"It is difficult to imagine the life after death," he said, chatting gaily. "Probably the best thing to do is to regard it as a continuation of the one we know with the same processes of growth and change until, eventually, we forget our life and associations on this earth, just as old people tend to forget their childhood experiences."

His Excellency who was a brother of the late Queen Mary and a soldier by profession muttered, "Yes, yes, probably." He obviously was shaken. He had been chosen by Mr. King to be Governor General of Canada and it made him nervous to learn that his Prime Minister was receiving advice from extra-mundane sources.

"Good God," he exclaimed when his staff explained why they had tried to shush him, 'is that where the man gets his policies?"

Having an open mind about the occult and being inquisitive by nature, I later managed to turn several conversations with Mr. King to this subject. Once, especially, when we were crossing the Atlantic to Europe, he talked freely about his beliefs and experiences as we walked the deck.

"If one believes in God and a life after death," he said, "it is inevitable that one must believe that the spirits of those who have gone take an interest in the people and places they loved during their lives on earth.

It is the matter of communication that is difficult. For myself I have found that the method of solitary, direct, communion is best. After my father and mother died I felt terribly alone. But I also felt that they were near me. Almost accidentally I established contact by talking to them as if they were present and soon I began to get replies."

These and other things that the Prime Minister said to me at different times came back to my mind as, on that June evening, I drove up the Kingsmere road and was reminded by a sign that the estate of Moorside, which Mr. King had left to the Canadian people in his will, lay just ahead.

It is a beautiful place. There are 550 acres of woodland and clearings, through most of which everyone is free to wander at will. A little stream with a waterfall flows through it down to the valley below. Mr. King accumulated it almost acre by acre, adding steadily in his methodical way, to the original lot he had bought when he first came to Ottawa at the beginning of the century. His quick temper seldom flashed more hotly than when he discovered that some neighbor had sold a parcel of land without giving him a chance to buy. Adding to his estate became a passion with the future Prime Minister. There he loved to receive visitors and also to be alone.

In buying the land Mr. King showed his Scottish shrewdness. But the building of the "ruins" was a perfect example of that romantic daftness that sometimes bewitches the supposedly hard-headed Scot. The direction sign now set up for tourists calls them 'ruins' but the uninformed must wonder what they once were. There were doorways and windows, a fireplace, a row of columns, which Mr. King called the cloisters, coats of arms carved in stone, bits and pieces of the old Parliament Buildings, the mint, banks and private houses all built into an artistic enough and wholly whimsical suggestion of a ruined castle. Somehow, perhaps because the surroundings with outcrop rock and pine are so fitting, they escape being silly.

On that evening there were no other visitors. The air was clear and cool. I sat down on a bench beside the ruins and thought about the strange little man who loved his hill-top home so clearly. I suppose I was in what I called a receptive mood. Although I had not then read it I was following the instructions in that letter from which I already have quoted, to "be still and listen and feel."

I became conscious that I was not alone. Someone sat on the park bench beside me.

There were no sighs, groans and lightning flashes such as mark a spirit's arrival on the Shakespearian stage. There was, if anything, a deeper peace. Through a fold in the hills I could see a stretch of the broad Ottawa Valley. I tried to concentrate on it and keep contact with the normal but the presence on the bench would not be denied.

Without turning my head, for somehow I feared to look, I said as naturally as I could, "Good evening, Mr. King."

In that warm tone which always marked his conversation the voice of Mr.King replied, "Good evening, Philip. I am so glad you spoke to me."

That surprised me. "I was thinking of you," I muttered.

"Oh, yes," he replied. "I knew that. But one of the rules which govern our conduct on this side is that we are like the children and must not speak unless we are spoken to. I suppose it is a good rule because it would be very disturbing if we went around talking to people. The sad thing is that so few of them ever talk to us."

Here I think I should say that the reader must decide for himself whether or not he believes this story. It puzzles me greatly.

"I suppose," I said, or I think I said, resuming the conversation, 'that we are just a bit scared. You know how hard it is to speak into a dark, empty room."

"That certainly is a difficulty for many people," Mr. King said. "But the room is never really empty. It is often filled with lonely ones who would like to be spoken to. They must, however, be called by name, confidently, affectionately, not challenged to declare themselves."

"Your name," I said, "must often be so mentioned in this lovely place you bequeathed to the Canadian people."

"Oh, yes, mentioned," he said. I glanced at him and seemed to see his eyes sparkle as they did in life, for he had a great deal of puckish humor. "But between being mentioned and being addressed by name, as you addressed me, there is a great deal of difference. I have heard things about my character, motives, political actions and even my personal appearance and habits that have made me laugh so loudly I thought I must break the sound barrier. And I have heard things about myself, too, that have made me shrink."

In the evening silence I had the sensation of being suspended in time and space as the quiet voice went on. "There are things that I said and did that I could regret but, on this side, we soon learn to have no regrets. Life would be meaningless if we did not all make mistakes, and eternity intolerable if we spent it regretting them."

He paused and I thought he looked at me quizzically. "By the way," he said, "Do you still write for the *New York Times*?"

When I said that I had retired he chuckled. "But still," he said, "I think I had better not give indiscreet answers to your questions."

I asked several but he answered with the same skill as marked his replies to questions in the House of Commons and at meetings with the press, divulging nothing. It was I who was the interviewed. He was eager for news and it surprised me then, as it does now, that he seemed not to know fully what was happening in the world. The dead, I discovered, are not omniscient. Or perhaps what we think important is not important to them.

We talked of the development of Canada, of housing and new enterprises like the St. Lawrence Seaway. "My successor has been lucky," Mr. King said. That was as far as he went in any personal reference. "Canada has been very prosperous. I hope it will continue to be so. But you cannot expect good times always. It is adversity that proves the real value of men and nations."

The conversation drifted to the international scene, to philosophic discussion of forms of government, of the balance between Liberty and Authority, the growth and decay of nations and of systems. I cannot tell how long it lasted but I noticed that the sickle moon was getting brighter. I mentioned the time, fumbling for my watch.

"Time," said Mr. King, "I had almost forgotten about time. I suppose I spend a great deal of time up here. There is so much beauty and peace. I gave it to the Canadian people but in a way I have preserved it for myself. It is good to have some familiar, well-loved place to spend 'time' in, until one gets used to eternity."

We both rose from the bench — or at least I did. When I looked at him, as I then did for the first time directly, he seemed just as I had known him in life, just as when I had talked with him once at this very spot.

"I think you told me once that you are Scottish born and a wee bit 'fey'," he said. "It's a good thing to be. We have two worlds. Those people who think their world is the only one, and who take it and themselves too seriously, have a very dull time. Do come back and talk with me again."

I muttered words of thanks and then, following the habit of a lifetime, stretched out my hand to bid goodbye. He was not there.

Source: Percy J. Philip, "I Talked with Mackenzie King's Ghost," *Fate Magazine*, Dec. 1955.

8. My Conversation with Mackenzie King's Ghost By Percy J. Philip Ex-*New York Times* Correspondent

So many people have asked me to tell them "the real truth" about my recent "interview" with the late Prime Minister Mackenzie King on the park bench at Kingsmere, Que., that I am glad to have the opportunity offered me by *Liberty*, to fill in the background and correct some misunderstandings, of the "ghost story" which I told over the CBC network last September 24.

Perhaps I should begin by saying that in Scotland, where I was born, we believe in ghosts. My father, who was a minister of the Church of Scotland, told me how his father had come to him in dreams, and on the edge of sleep, so vividly he could not afterwards believe that it was not real. Even more oddly, though he died at the age of 86 when I was three years old, my gaunt old grandfather, wrapped in his homespun plaid, has paid me several visits. Afterwards, I could not say definitely whether I had been asleep or awake. But the whole conversation, even to the old man's slight Aberdeenshire accent, was so vivid that I was positive it had actually taken place.

And that is how it was in my conversation with Mr. King on the park bench among the ruins at Kingsmere last June.

What the explanation may be of such phenomena I do not claim to understand. They may be due to psychic influence, to a stimulated imagination, or to that subconscious working of the mind which happens in dreams.

Yet there is no incompatibility between being a Christian and church-goer, as Mr. King was, and being a searcher into the mystery of the hereafter. During his life, we had several discussions on the fascinating subject, and it came to me as a surprise when, after his death, it was "revealed" in a magazine article that he had been a practising spiritualist. I thought everybody knew about it.

Like many others of his friends, I resented this, perhaps unintentional, exposure of Mr. King to ridicule. Perhaps I should have been warned not to touch such a sensitive subject. There may be no witches in Canada, but there are witch-hunters.

Still I have been a reporter all my life, and I could not resist trying to write an account of that strange experience at Kingsmere. I did it with the greatest care.

I offered what I had written to a national Canadian magazine — not *Liberty* — but it was courteously rejected. I was told later it had gone to the fiction department and had not been regarded as very good fiction.

So I redrafted it for broadcasting. I thought that my Scottish voice might convey my meaning with more subtlety than the cold printed word. I stress its unusual character, I called the talk *Fantasio*. As I would have a much wider audience on the air, I strengthened the warnings that it should not be taken too literally, writing that I was not sure that I believed my story myself, and prefacing my account of the "facts" with the conditional phrase — "If in the mystery of life and the hereafter, there are such things as facts."

That, it seemed to me, provided the key to the story. It was a mystery, and a pleasant one.

The CBC editors, to whom the script was submitted, read it understandingly, and accepted it for broadcasting.

Listeners from one end of the country to another seem also to have understood. Two of Mr. King's literary executors, who have had access to all his private papers, and a former member of his cabinet, were enthusiastic about the portrait I had drawn of their old leader.

But when we come to the treatment of the story by the press, that is another matter.

It perhaps ill becomes one who has been a newspaper reporter all his life, and has undoubtedly made his full measure of mistakes of interpretation and even of fact, to be critical of his colleagues who may fall into error.

I find, however, that some account of how my broadcast was handled by the press is necessary for the proper understanding of the Legend of the Bench at Kingsmere.

That legend has already travelled far beyond Canada. It has brought more than 200 letters, from every province and from many states of the American union. Every weekend, and even during the week, hundreds of visitors have been flocking up to Moorside and arguing hotly whether or not the "ghost" really appeared. The delegates of the Colombo plan conference in Ottawa have carried the story to the ends of the earth. Political commentators have seized on it as a peg on which to hang pontifical articles. Collins, in the Montreal *Gazette*, lifted it to a high point of humor with his cartoon of Prime Minister St. Laurent sitting on the bench among the ruins, looking pensively upward and asking: "Have you anything to say to *me?*"

But the condensed version of the talk circulated by The Canadian Press was not so well inspired. Probably it was the first time that that news agency had ever put a ghost story on its wires. Certainly it was the fist time a CP staff member, in the Ottawa bureau, had ever been asked to provide one.

It was no excuse that the poor fellow had not heard the broadcast. The first thing to do, of course, was to secure the text. There was none available at the CBC studios, as the broadcast had been recorded. I live at Aylmer, Ont., 10 miles from Ottawa, and apparently the CP Ottawa bureau is not equipped to send an intelligent reporter so far to get a story.

I soon found it was impossible to get the facts, nuances, qualifications, suggestions, anecdotes and imponderables into position by telephone. After a struggle, I consented to drive in myself with the text. I might, I thought, be able to keep the story from running wild.

My efforts were wasted. The CP had asked for a ghost story, and the more I insisted that the subject was delicate and the treatment whimsical, the more certain I became that the ghost story I had told over the CBC network, and the one that would be printed, would have little resemblance.

What a fool I had been. I had thought that my broadcast might stir some interest, but I had definitely under-estimated its impact on the ghost-hungry newspaper mind. It made the front pages all across Canada, pushing aside the argument then in progress between Mr. St. Laurent and Quebec Premier Maurice Duplessis.

There were odd little changes. Whereas I had said Mr. King talked to me, the headlines ran that I had talked with Mr. King. The title word, *Fantasio*, became "Fantastic," which is quite different. Sentences were transposed and others, which had seemed so important to me, were entirely omitted.

Not a single newspaper published the text of the talk. Even those, to which a copy had been sent in advance, preferred to publish the CBC version, rather than go to the trouble of writing their own.

The telephone began ringing. Was it true? Argument was warm.

Editors began telegraphing their Ottawa correspondents: Had Philip gone "crackers"? One wit, of sorts, telephoned to ask what brand of whisky I drank.

At 8:30 a.m., on the following Sunday, one of the most enterprising and joyous of my colleagues burst into my cottage, shouting gaily: "The question is — is it true, or is it not true?"

There were others who did not bother even to telephone but began writing freely, interviewing parsons, chauffeurs, CBC officials and residents of Kingsmere.

In the press, the skeptics certainly outnumbered the believers, but the latter were much more industrious in writing private letters. Two spiritualists told of recent conversations with Mr. King who, they said, had confirmed my story. I shall not call them witnesses.

Source: Percy J. Philip, "My Conversation with Mackenzie King's Ghost," *Liberty*, January 1955.

9. Canadian Spiritualism: Racket or Religion? By Frank Rasky

I sat on a park bench at Kingsmere, Que., one crisp afternoon a few weeks ago with Percy J. Philip, retired Ottawa correspondent for the *New York Times*. But though we beseeched the skies and cried aloud to the wind whispering through the pine trees, the ghost of Mackenzie King failed to materialize for us.

Instead, up the grassy knoll in front of us popped the very corporeal, but astonished, faces of two living women. I was amused because their husbands, ironically, had been the Liberal Prime Minister's bitterest political enemies before his death in July, 1950. One of the ladies was Mrs. George Drew, wife of Canada's Progressive-Conservative Party leader. Our other visitor was Mrs. George McCullagh, widow of the late publisher of Toronto's Tory *Telegram* and *Globe & Mail*.

It was the first time they'd ever visited King's 550-acre Summer estate, the ladies explained embarrassedly. They'd come to inspect the now-famous park bench where the *Times* journalist claimed, over the CBC last Fall, to have exchanged ghostly repartee with King. Naturally, the ladies were jolted to stroll upon Philip himself beside me, as he tried once again to conjure up the Prime Minister's wraith.

We all had a good laugh over the unexpected meeting. It was, we agreed, rather like some extra-terrestrial, park bench version of *Brigadoon*.

"Eerie enough almost," said Mrs. Drew light-heartedly, "to make you believe in spirits."

Despite Mrs. Drew's jocular attitude, and Philip's explanation (see accompanying story) that his conversation with King was written in a whimsical vein, there are at least 500,000 Canadians whose belief in ghosts is no joke at all. Indeed, McClelland & Stewart will publish this year a book, *Exploring the Supernatural*, by R. S. Lambert, which suggests that Canada today is brimming with ghosts....

Lambert is not surprised by the prevalence of ghost stories in Canada. "Canada's lonely farms and unexplored wildernesses help to breed mystery and stretch the imagination," he says. "The interest of Mackenzie King in spiritualism is an example of what may lie hidden under the normal, outer rind of Canadian hard-headedness...."

Publicity accorded to Philip's exchange of ghostly gossip with King has, too, stimulated Canadians to use these cosmic Western Union messengers....

The National Spiritualist Association...flourishes largely in western Canada. Its fountainhead is British Columbia, the only Canadian province licensing its 12 reverend mediums to perform marriage ceremonies....

Actual president of the NSA is Rev. Samuel H. Daniels of New Westminster, B.C. He is a granite-jawed, London-born faith healer of 55, who estimates that one-tenth of Canada's population are spiritualist adherents. "I have contacted scores of influential world figures in my private séances," he told me. "People like Sir Arthur Conan Doyle, Sir Oliver Lodge and Nurse Edith Cavell."

Rev. Daniels vies with other Canadian mediums in buttressing the validity of Philip's conversation with Mackenzie King's ghost.

"My wife, Rev. Louise Daniels, who is a medium of psychic research in Burnaby, B.C., actually knew it in *advance*," he firmly insists. "It happened on a lovely afternoon in October, 1953. While we were taking photographs on a visit to the ruins of Kingsmere, Mr. King communicated with my wife. He expressed his difficulty in getting a message through to the world.

"We suggested to his spirit that a newspaper reporter, of sound judgment and sincerity, would be the best medium for this purpose. Yet neither my wife nor I have ever met Mr. Philip!...."

Is Canadian spiritualism a racket or a bona fide religion? It's hard to say....

Are Canada's mediums, with their sensitive talents for telepathy, really able to commune with Mackenzie King's ghost? In his lifetime, King claimed to have communed with the spirits of Abraham Lincoln, Sir Wilfrid Laurier, Franklin D. Roosevelt, his mother, and his Irish terrier, Pat. Now that he is dead himself, the enigma of his own ghostly eloquence can be answered only by Mackenzie King's wraith, hovering on an astral sphere somewhere over the Gatineau Hills of Kingsmere, Que., and undoubtedly chuckling gleefully at the fuss below stirred up by his old friend, Percy Philip.

Source: Frank Rasky, "Canadian Spiritualism: Racket or Religion?" *Liberty*, January 1955 (excerpted).

10. Percy J. Philip "For 33 Years He Covered Canada, France" (c) *New York Times Service*

Ottawa, Nov. 9 — Percy J. Philip, 70, correspondent for *The New York Times* in Canada and Paris for 33 years, died here today of heart disease.

Mr. Philip had lived here since his retirement in January, 1954. He leaves his wife Marguerite.

Born on July 12, 1886, at the manse of Kells in Galloway, Scotland, the son of a Presbyterian minister, he rejected his father's advice to become a clergyman, preferring to study medicine.

His bad heart, however, forced him to drop out of Edinburgh University. For a while, he was an assistant to Sir James Murray at Oxford University on compilation of the Oxford English dictionary. But this work, also, was too confining. He then lived in the English countryside, writing nature sketches for London newspapers and magazines.

Happening to be in Europe when the First World War broke out, he was taken on as a reporter for the *London Daily News*. He covered the fighting in Belgium, just managing to escape to the Netherlands on a barge ahead of the invading Germans.

Later in the war, he went to Paris as correspondent for several English papers, including the *Daily Mail*, *Daily News*, *Birmingham Post* and *Westminster Gazette*. He was still there when hired in 1920 to assist Edwin L. James, then head of *The New York Times* bureau in Paris. He was valuable because of his fluency in French and his knowledge of French politics.

Philip became head of the bureau in 1932, remaining there until the office was officially closed after the surrender of France to the Germans in 1940. He continued briefly in Vichy, temporary capital of unoccupied France, until transferred to Ottawa as Canadian correspondent for *The Times* in 1941.

He was president of the Ottawa Parliamentary Press Gallery in 1945.

Mr. Philip got wide Canadian publicity in 1954 when in a CBC broadcast entitled Fantasio he suggested he had had a conversation with his late friend Prime Minster Mackenzie King, who died in 1950. After his death it was revealed Mr. King had consulted spiritualists.

Intimates of the waggish Mr. Philip never were quite sure if he was pulling a country-wide spoof on radio listeners or if he believed he had talked to the shade of the former prime minister while sitting on a park bench in Mr. King's old country estate of nearby Kingsmere.

"I'm not sure that I believe it myself," he told his audience. "But it seemed so real at the time and not in the least unusual. It was indeed so real that it haunted me ever since. And like the Ancient Mariner, I have got to tell my tale."

He said to a reporter who asked him later if he was putting over a deliberate fantasy: "I don't know whether I was. I got to like the story more each day."

Indeed, the incident helped to publicize Kingsmere, where the following year Mr. Philip was one of the leading lights in a series of musical and theatrical events staged in a natural ourdoors amphitheatre on the Kingsmere grounds.

During his years in France, Philip became well acquainted with important French politicians and foreign diplomats. His connections got him inside the Chateau Cande near Tours for the marriage of the Duke of Windsor and Wallis Warfield Simpson in 1937. He was the only newspaperman among the hundreds there to get so close.

Philip wrote articles not only on French politics, but widely, also on the art and life of Paris and the provinces he knew so well. Sometimes he broadcast over the BBC. During his 13 years as *The Times* correspondent in Canada, and even after retirement, he continued his witty chats over the Canadian Broadcasting Corp. network.

One of these, made immediately after the raid by Canadian commandos on Dieppe, is still remembered. Mr. Philip had owned a summer villa at Dieppe and was able to describe the scene with moving eloquence.

After retirement, Mr. Philip continued occasional radio talks and did voluntary publicity work for the Victorian Order of Nurses. He was a member of the Order of the British Empire and the Legion of Honor for his services to Britain and France.

Source: "For 33 Years He Covered Canada, France," *The Globe and Mail*, 10 Nov. 1956.

11. Mackenzie King, Canada's Famed Prime Minister — or, How to Run a Country and Still Have Time For the Next World
By Arthur Myers

...not all writers were unsympathetic, or even skeptical, about King's psychic activities. One well-known member of the Ottawa press corps, Percy Philips, wrote articles and went on the CBC stating that in 1954 he had encountered the ghost of King and had had an extended conversation with him. Philip's journalistic credentials were impeccable; he had covered the Canadian government for the *New York Times* for some twenty-five years.

I called the *Times* foreign desk to try to find out something about Philip, but no one on duty that day had ever heard of him; after all, he dated back at least thirty years. But Victor Mackie, who had been chief of bureau in Ottawa for a group of newspapers, remembers Philip well.

"He was very dignified," Mackie told me, "very self-conscious about working for the *New York Times*. He let you know as soon [as] you met him that he worked for the *Times*. But he had a humorous glint in his eye. When he did this story we in the press gallery thought he was pulling our legs. We asked him what he had been drinking lately and he just passed it off. We in the gallery all treated it as a Philip pull-your-leg sort of thing. I don't know to this day whether he really saw a spectre of King or whether he just dreamed it up as a joke on a dull day."

Source: Arthur Myers, *Ghosts of the Rich and Famous* (Chicago: Contemporary Books, 1988), Chapter 20 (excerpt).

Sources

Every reasonable attempt has been made to contact the individual copyright owners of the selections included in this anthology. In not every instance has this proved to be possible. The editor and publisher hereby acknowledge their use of previously copyright passages written by the following authors: WILL R. BIRD: *Ghosts Have Warm Hands* (Toronto: The Ryerson Press, 1968). Excerpt reproduced courtesy of McGraw-Hill Ryerson Limited. FLORENCE LIDDELL: *The Flying Scotsman* (London: Quartet Books, 1981) written by Sally Magnusson. Permission requested. L.M. MONGOMERY: *The Selected Journals of L.M. Montgomery: Volume I: 1889-1910* (Toronto: Oxford University Press, 1985), edited by Mary Rubio and Elizabeth Waterston. Entries: Nov. 18, 1907; Dec. 14, 1907. Reprinted by permission of the University of Guelph. PERCY J. PHILIP: "I Talked with Mackenzie King's Ghost," *Fate Magazine*, Dec. 1955. "My Conversation with Mackenzie King's Ghost," *Liberty*, Jan. 1955. Permission requested. "My Conversation with Mackenzie King's Ghost," *Liberty*, Jan. 1955. Permission Requested. FRANK RASKY: "Canadian Spiritualism: Racket or Religion?" *Liberty*, Jan. 1955. Reprinted by permission of the author. BEN ROSE: "Spirit of Mackenzie King in Garden — Writer," *The Toronto Star*, 25 Sept. 1954. Reprinted by permission. GEORGE WOODCOCK: *Letter to the Past: An Autobiography* (Toronto: Fitzhenry & Whiteside, 1982) and *Beyond the Blue Mountains* (Toronto: Fitzhenry & Whiteside, 1987). Excerpts reproduced courtesy of the author and the publisher. Anonymous: "Ghostly Gossip on a Bench with Mackenzie King," CP Story, *The Globe and Mail*, 25 Sept. 1954. Reproduced by permission of Canadian Press. Anonymous: "Percy J. Philip: For 33 Years He Covered Canada, France." The New York Times Service, *The Globe and Mail*, 10 Nov. 1956. Copyright© 1956 The New York Times Company. Reprinted by permission.